The

# LIMITLESS APPROACH

LIFE BUSINESS INVESTMENT

THE LIMITLESS APPROACH



Published by Marcus Richmond Partners LLC March 2019

ISBN: 978-0-9987462-2-7

# The LIMITLESS APPROACH

LIFE BUSINESS INVESTMENT

BY MARCUS A. TURNER

ACKNOWLEDGMENTS

The world is a better place thanks to people who want to develop and lead others. What makes it even better are people who share the gift of their time to mentor future leaders. Thank you to everyone who strives to grow and help others grow. For the poets, philosophers, authors, artists, scientists, and great thinkers, your work played a part in setting my soul ablaze. There are no original ideas, and everything that comes from me has been stimulated by another. It is the business version of The Lion King song, "Circle of Life."

To all the individuals I have had the opportunity to lead, be led by, or watch their leadership from afar. From everyone I have ever encountered, life is a sum of experiences whether good or bad and without those there wouldn't be anything to say, so I thank you too.

I want to thank:

I want to thank God most of all, because without God I wouldn't be in this position.

To my wife Felicia and son Jeremy, I love you both with all my heart and I thank you immensely for all your support.

My grandmas, RIP.

My mom and auntie, thank you for your endless love and support. I love you.

My aunties and uncles.

My stepfather, who is only that in name; he fathered me and took on the responsibility of raising a son he didn't spawn. For that, I will always be grateful.

My dad, for donating the sperm that made me, and later, he gave me his love and the opportunity to get to know him. I am grateful for the time I had with you; it was truly a blessed experience. RIP…

All my brothers, sisters, and cousins… To the Kirk, Turner and Richmond families, you all have contributed to me immeasurably. Thank you…

To my team, Linette Smith, Pat McElya, Thomas Goines, and Dexter Samuels, you all have been with me since the beginning of this phase of my entrepreneurial endeavors. I truly appreciate all you do in making me look fabulous.

I want to say thank you to all of you for being the inspiration and foundation for The Limitless Approach: Life- Business- Investments.

# TABLE OF CONTENTS

# INTRODUCTION

I believe in a different kind of wealth management, a practice that is truly integrated with your life, not absent or separate from it. In any market-related function it will appear to be fraught with uncertainty, and to the untrained eye, a game of chance. However, this is only true for the individual who has not begun the process of mastering himself. If the individual is unstable, so will be his choices, decisions, and life. However, for the man who has mastered himself, who has to learn to be stable independently of others, he will bring the order and stability to all situations that he is intimately involved with. Whether it be concerning life, business, or investment, this is similar to the story in the Bible where Jesus was asleep in the stern of the boat in the midst of a violent storm. The disciples were at a fever pitch and were scared for their lives. They awakened a frustrated Jesus. "Master, do you care that we may perish?"

He arose, and He rebuked the wind, stating, "Peace, be still," and the wind ceased and there was a great calm. Where did the calm come from? Well it came from inside of Him. Only the peaceful can distill peace, only the wise, wisdom, the violent, violence, and so on and so on. It's the law of the Earth; we can only produce what we are. So many choose wealth managers based off so many diverse reasons. Many stem from education levels and whom they know or their previous quarters' returns. Guy Spier, in his book The Education of a Value Investor, noted:

> Did my education fail me? Or, even worse, did I fail my education? There's a larger question to be asked here, too, since I'm also a microcosm of my peer group. Why did so many highly educated people from elite business schools and privileged background contribute to and exacerbate the financial crisis of 2008-2009? Did our education fail us? Or did we fail our education? These questions haven't been answered adequately by the prestigious universities that groomed all these high-powered creators of economic mayhem.

One success has never been purely predicated on the quality of an education one might receive, unless that knowledge includes the importance of the principles that govern life. See to be smart, intelligent and have an excellent education is terrific. However, to have these attributes with poor character is dangerous. If I could respond to Mr. Spier, I would explain the dangers of giving unregulated weapons of mass destruction to a bunch of overeducated, prideful, materialistic, amoral fools would be equivalent to handing a baby a loaded gun. To wield significant power is desirable by all. However, considerable power requires excellent character, discipline, compassion, and wisdom; these things are of more importance than smarts or an education. Wealth Managers do need an education of the mind, but what is paramount is that they have an education of the heart. Any institution or government flirts with disaster when they empower the minds and intellect but neglect the character. "A little that a righteous man hath is better than the riches of many wicked." Therefore, the focus should not be to attain or grow money without an intense focus on improving the individual first. If we continue to focus on the attainment and the growth of money we are driving the nails into our own coffins. Throughout history, this thinking has destroyed countless individuals, families, institutions, governments, and countries. "Beloved, I wish above all things that thou may prosper and be in health, even as thy soul prospers." It is a direct correlation between wealth and the ability to manage that wealth by, wisdom, knowledge, understanding and overall character.

However, many people who try their hand at investing soon realize they can only produce what they are. Unless they have found a way to cheat the process temporarily, but over time that will be revealed. However, if you get people to understand that ultimately what matters is who you are, and who you are will determine your success in the market, as well as in life. Are you a person of character? Are you truthful and do you deal in truth? Are you a man or woman of discipline and peace? Are you a student of life and the principles that govern it? The market, like life, will disclose your deficiencies. Money is indeed an extension of who we are and the skills and abilities we possess. If you take five dollars and give it to ten different people to invest, you will get ten different results, because money is neutral and will eventually rise and fall based on the understanding, insight, and skill of the owner.

In this book we will take a look at our capitalistic history, and how it has manifested into our current social, economic, and political environment. What are the positives and negatives of these environments, and how have they and how can they continue to determine your outcome? In the second half of the book, we will examine many principles that undergird robust financial health, and how accumulating wealth must be seen through a healthy paradigm, one that does not teach that your survival is dependent of the destruction of another's.

# THE TRUTH IS

> "I believe that unarmed truth and unconditional love will have the final word in reality. This is why right, temporarily defeated, is stronger than evil triumphant."
>
> —Martin Luther King Jr.

What is truth, and why is it important? Many historians have wrestled with these questions. Whether we are talking about great men of faith, philosophers, writers, poets, intellectuals, and scientists, they all understood that any nation or citizen who doesn't have a high regard for truth will inevitably find themselves lost within the maze of confusion. I have often found myself tripped up over particular truths that I failed to acknowledge concerning myself. There were situations where there would be different people and environments, and I would somehow encounter the same issue over and over again. My experiences became like a roller coaster; I continued making the same errors. I was the living example of insanity, doing the same thing repeatedly and expecting a different result. After some time had passed and frustration had set in, I needed to uncover the problem. First, I began to dissect every person involved in these situations, and I readily concluded that they were all heathens and they needed a one-way pass directly to hell. Finally, as the sun often rises in the morning, I had the answer: it' was these clever, unscrupulous deceivers who were causing me all of these problems. However I moved away from those heathens, I was sure life would be different. About a year later, I was staring at a similar situation all over again. At that point, I realized that I was the common denominator; in every case when the players and locations changed I was the only consistent occurrence. Immediately, I felt like I was going to throw up, I was sick to my stomach. Could it be me that was causing all of my issues? But I am a good person, I thought. I go to church, I pray, I have tried to do everything I was taught to do. What if the people who taught me were somehow in error? I soon realized that perhaps some of those things that I believed to be true were not true at all. From that moment forward I began to question everything I had learned and that I thought I knew. Did I understand what I was taught, or was I doing more of what I saw than what was preached? You know, at times your parent says: do as I say, not as I do. I was living my truth, but was it the truth.

For example, I believed that opposites attract, but they do not. Likes attract. I began to understand that you attract what you are, not what you wish to be, that your current reality is a total of the seeds you have sown. I was the problem. These unscrupulous, clever deceivers, those heathens, mirrored a part myself, and I attracted them. Therefore, to change my situation, to get off this roller coaster, I must change.

This proved to be true, I began to seek out more truth, and as I found that truth and applied it, my situation changed for the better. Today, I love truth, no matter how painful or difficult to accept. I know in the end, I will be better off receiving it and applying it to my life. Later, as I continued to mature, this pursuit of truth became a part of my daily life. In every situation my number one question was: what do I know to be true? It was amazing how that question added clarity to every choice or decision that I needed to make; I quickly realized how much I did not know. It was also an awakening; the more I sought truth, the more I noticed how many chose not to. How comfortable many were in believing something that someone told them, or they heard from some news station or a random person they met at the airport. It was quite shocking and to think, I, up to that point I had lived much of my life doing the same. However, quickly I saw how my new path began to alter relationships and to change my tolerance for what I saw as foolishness. I was not judging them; I was judging me, because I had been an honorary, card-carrying member of the "Foolishness Club." But I was different and there was no going back to my past reality. The light bulb had been lit, and though it cost me some relationships, it was a small price to pay for my newfound freedom. Today, I often listen because many have purposely chosen their blindness, and they'd rather deceive themselves than to face the truth. How do I know? Well, I have lived that reality.

> "When I despair, I remember that all through history the way of truth and love have always won. There have been tyrants and murderers, and for a time, they can seem invincible, but in the end, they always fall. Think of it—always."
>
> —Gandhi

> "I'm for truth, no matter who tells it. I'm for justice, no matter who it is for or against. I'm a human being, first and foremost, and as such I'm for whoever and whatever benefits humanity as a whole."
>
> —Malcolm X

Some years ago I read this story; the subject matter made a profound impression on me. It begins in ancient Greece, and its main character is a historical figure by the name of Socrates, a philosopher of great wisdom who sincerely valued knowledge. One day an old classmate approached Socrates and said, "Do you know what I just heard about your friend?"

"Please wait before telling me," the philosopher responded. "Before telling me anything I'd like you to pass a little test. It's called the Triple Filter Test."

"Triple filter?"

"That's right," Socrates continued. "Before you lecture me concerning my dear friend, it would be expedient to take a moment and filter what you're going to say. That's why I call it the Triple Filter Test. The first filter is Truth. Have you made sure that what you are about to tell me is true?"

"No," the man said, "Actually I just heard about it and—"

"All right," said Socrates. "So you don't know if it's true or not. Now let's try the second filter, the filter of Goodness. Is what you are about to tell me about my friend something good?"

"No, on the contrary…"

"So,"

Socrates continued, "you want to tell me something bad about him, but you're not certain it's true. You may still pass the test, though, because there's one filter left: the filter of Usefulness. Is what you want to tell me about my friend going to be useful to me?"

"No, not really ..."

"Well," concluded Socrates, "if what you want to tell me is not true nor good nor even useful, why tell it to me at all?"

> "Above all, don't lie to yourself. The man who lies to himself and listens to his lie comes to the point that he cannot distinguish the truth within him, or around him, and so loses all respect for him and others. And having no respect, he ceases to love."
>
> —Fyodor Dostoyevsky, The Brothers Karamazov

TRUTH is paramount for everyone who wishes to improve the quality of their life, not just their truth but also "the" truth. The truth is the absolute unchanging reality, which is a building block or principle that governs life. Your truth is an assumed fact that you have given the same power as truth, over your life, even though it's nothing more than an opinion. The problem is this belief that has been accepted as your truth is a lie and you are actually in deception. Therefore every lesson, concept, business, or relationship they place on that deception will fail. Many have built their life on the sand of deception instead of on the unchanging, solid foundation of truth.

One is not to feel isolated in this occurrence. We all have these areas in our life where we have the assumed truths that become like mine fields in our lives. We sincerely believe that we are in truth but are actually in deception, building more and more minefields that are certain to explode. The idea is to begin to evaluate our belief system and to remove our ego so that we can discover these areas of dysfunction that are aligned with deception and begin the work of discovering the truth. It is not an easy process and will require a level of humility that very few possess. However, if it were easy, everyone would do it. This is the work of champions—to face the psychosis of infallibility with the serum of truth, moving humanity forward while destroying the shackles that ignorance enforces. In order to be sincerely true to ourselves, we must forge a relationship with the pursuit of truth.

This book is intended for the individual who has chosen to leave his current reality and seek something of greater consequence, for all who would like to release the boundaries from around their existence and walk into the boundless, endless reality of limitless living. What I am speaking of is simple: would you like to be liberated from the boundaries that have been established over your life? To seize control over your life and never again feel that your life is happening to you, but you and no one else are co-creating it? Well, this kind of living is a journey that starts with a choice, a choice that only you can make. What is that choice? You must first decide to have a relationship with the truth, not just your truth but "the" truth. No matter how agonizing or distressing it may be, it is the truth that will liberate, if you are willing to accept it. Otherwise, you will build a similar prison to that which you are currently living in, which is fortified with bad ideas and principles that are contrary to the truth.

> "It is an illusion that youth is happy, an illusion of those who have lost it; but the young know they are wretched for they are full of the truthless ideal which has been instilled into them, and each time they come in contact with the real, they are bruised and wounded. It looks as if they were victims of a conspiracy; for the books they read, ideal by the necessity of selection, and the conver-

> sation of their elders, who look back upon the past through a rosy haze of forgetfulness, prepare them for an unreal life. They must discover for themselves that all they have read and all they have been told are lies, lies; and each discovery is another nail driven into the body on the cross of life."
>
> —W. Somerset Maugham, Of Human Bondage

I will be introducing some concepts that will challenge the status quo. It will likely oppose many of the ideas that you have already concluded are truths. However, please understand that this is a part of the overall process. To eliminate sacred cows will be painful and the ah-ha moments of revelation will be joyous, but any transformation or transition process will require patience and some discomfort. Also, remember this is your choice, so you cannot expect others to agree with your new perspective. The world is full of those with "Doubting Thomas" syndrome, where only by seeing will they believe. Be prepared to proceed on this journey alone if that's what this decision demands. Remember, if it were easy everyone would do it.

If this is not a choice you are willing to make, everything else I say will appear strange, out of touch, and frustrating. So, please give this book to someone else who desires to accomplish something more with this extraordinary gift of life.

> "It is always the false that makes you suffer, the false desires and fears, the false values and ideas, the false relationships between people. Abandon the false, and you are free of pain; truth makes happy, truth liberates."
>
> —Nisargadatta Maharaja

The truth is that we must be appreciative of every single breath we take, no matter how dire our situation may appear. Life is a gift, and all of us have an adequate supply of everything we need to become our best selves. It is not about fame, fortune, or worldly success, what it is about are those things that nourish and fulfill our soul—those things such as love, respect, and consideration, which we all have in unlimited supply. Even if these things are not coming from the people we desire to receive them from, just look a little bit closer. There's someone who is lovingly respecting and supporting you and many others that are prepared to do the same.

As I reminisce about my life, through various difficult phases, there was always a coach, teacher, neighbor, social worker, adoptive parent, and so on, who gave me more than I could ask. While some offered themselves unwillingly or by default, there were those who gave of themselves willingly. Sure, there were those whom I may have expected these things from which I didn't get. However, there was always someone else to fill that gap. Over the years, through the seasons and location changes of my journey, there was always a kind soul that stepped up to fill voids that were left empty. All I can be is grateful. I am confident that in this life, no matter what happens, there will be someone who will show up when I need them most, and there will be a lonely soul that I must show up for when a gap appears in their life. It does not matter who you are, and the intricate details of how you got there, or who your parents were, or what they did. All that matters is that you are here and because you have breath, you are necessary, and you are enough. So, appreciate life and every breath you take, because your breath alone is proof that there is work you must do.

> "Our deepest fear is not that we are inadequate. Our deepest fear is that we are powerful beyond measure. It is our light, not our darkness that most frightens us. We ask ourselves, who am I to be brilliant, gorgeous, talented, fabulous? Actually, who are you not to be? You are a child of God. Your playing small doesn't serve the world. There's nothing enlightened about shrinking so that other people won't feel insecure around you. We are all meant to shine, as children do. We were born to make manifest the glory of God that is within us. It's not just in some of us; it's in everyone. And as we let our own light shine, we subconsciously give other people permission to do the same. As we're liberated from our own fear, our presence automatically liberates others."
>
> —Marianne Williamson

The truth is that your environment does not happen to you. You happen to your environment. We are not to live from the outside in but from the inside out. Outside of us is the temporal, the natural. Inside of us is the eternal, the limitless, and the endless universe. We shouldn't look outside of ourselves to find out who we are but inside ourselves. Your purpose is seared into your soul and no matter what the obstacle, once you know your purpose then you will change the environment, and reshape your story. We are more powerful than we can fathom. One idea supported by belief and work can change the trajectory of the world. Ultimately, you have created your current environment, which means it can be recreated no matter how impossible it may seem. All things are possible that were once thought to be impossible. Nothing is impossible to the individual who believes.

> "Impossible is just a big word thrown around by small men who find it easier to live in the world they've been given than to explore the power they have to change it. Impossible is not a fact. It's an opinion. Impossible is not a declaration. It's a dare. Impossible is potential. Impossible is temporary. Impossible is nothing."
>
> —Muhammad Ali

Today, begin to reshape your environment based on the purpose that is seared into your soul. Nothing happens to you; you happen to it. It has never been about what happens; it is how you respond to it that will eventually dictate the narrative. Change is different from transformation. You can change your hairstyle. However, your hair will eventually return to its previous form. A lie can only stand for a season but the truth is forever. Change is temporary; it's a lie. However, an authentic conversion is for life.

> "People think that a liar gains a victory over his victim. What I've learned is that a lie is an act of self-abdication, because one surrenders one's reality to the person to whom one lies, making that person one's master, condemning oneself from then on to faking the sort of reality that person's view requires to be faked...The man who lies to the world is the world's slave from then on...There are no white lies, there is only the blackest of destruction, and a white lie is the blackest of all."
>
> —Ayn Rand, Atlas Shrugged

Just think of yourself as a seed. Take an apple seed, once planted in its soil, given proper care, which includes water and sunlight. That seed will eventually die, and its hard outer shell will give way to its pure transforming power that was trapped inside. The apple seed has now reproduced itself in a different form. It has been transformed with no chance of returning to its previous state, but the seed of its beginning is forever present. The apple does not resemble its seed; it is unrecognizable from where it began. We are to be the same; we must allow the hard outer shell to die so that the genuine gift of our being, which we are authentically, can reveal itself to the world.

> "Over the years, I have come to realize that the greatest trap in our life is not success, popularity, or power, but self-rejection. Success, popularity, and power can indeed present a great temptation, but their seductive quality often comes from the way they are part of the much larger temptation to self-rejection. When we have come to believe in the voices that call us worthless and unlovable, then success, popularity, and power are easily perceived as attractive solutions. The real trap, however, is self-rejection. As soon as someone accuses me or criticizes me, as soon as I am rejected, left alone, or abandoned, I find myself thinking, "Well, that proves once again that I am a nobody." ... [My dark side says,] I am no good... I deserve to be pushed aside, forgotten, rejected, and abandoned. Self-rejection is the greatest enemy of the spiritual life because it contradicts the sacred voice that calls us the "Beloved." Being the Beloved constitutes the core truth of our existence."
>
> —Henri J.M. Noun

The truth is that each and every one is granted a gift of boundless potential. We are a unique species, which can affect two realities simultaneously: the spiritual and the natural. These parallel realities are both governed by the power of choice—your choice. We must choose, and believe in that choice, which is why predicting where the next person will be born, or who will change the world, is unlikely. It is not determined by the external, but by the internal. At some point, the individual must decide to shed that outer shell of containment and dream the big dream to hope against hope. We all have the power, but will we choose a life of sacrifice, work, and selflessness? What will you decide? Choose truth, which yields freedom and life. By not selecting, by default, you have made a choice and that choice will be your truth, but will it be "the" truth?

> "The truth will set you free. But not until it is finished with you."
>
> —David Foster Wallace, Infinite Jest

# THE AMERICAN EXPERIMENT

"In the beginning all the world was America."

I remember when I was in grade school and the childlike struggles I encountered, attempting to understand myself, our family, and how we all fit inside of this vast American culture. I wanted to be seen not literally but deeply. I had this deep desire to be relevant, even though I was this shy and quiet kid. Now, this is years before I wrestled with the real questions that later appeared, like, who am I, and what am I to do in this world. Back then it was simple, all I wanted was to be loved, heard and understood. No one told me that I would spend the remainder of my life trying to unpack exactly what that means.

In school my teachers begin to pour information on us about who we were as Americans. The instructors did this by teaching American history. For me it was so confusing. There seemed to be so many contradictions. I was raised Christian, and sure the Golden Rule and the Ten Commandments were what we were taught to live by. In school this was re-enforced by the teachers, and I was thrilled to find out that our Founding Fathers were Christian. We learned that Christopher Columbus discovered a land by accident that already had inhabitants (I am still trying to figure that out), yet he claimed to discover a new land.

Eventually, a group of Christians who were from England felt that freedom of religion was being compromised by the government, and decided to come to this new land. This new land would be founded on freedom and Christian values. Before long, these Christian immigrants had stolen the land from the Indians (Thou shalt not steal). They befriended them, only to learn how to survive on the Indians' land (Thou shalt not bear false witness against thy neighbor or lie) and invited them to a celebration where shortly after they proceeded to kill them (Thou shalt not kill), to take total control of their land (Thou shalt not covet thy neighbor's house, nor his farm, nor his cattle, nor anything that is his). Eventually, because these Christians could not manage or work the land they had stolen, they decided to steal men, women, and children from their home country and enslave them to work the stolen land, ultimately declaring them sub-human and lazy. To justify these unspeakable sins, they declared "manifest destiny," in other words, God's Will. Hopefully, you can now see how American history confused a young kid like myself. Later, there were many more things that baffled my young mind about this American Experiment.

From the beginning, when the Pilgrims and Puritans first set foot on American soil, they arrived with their hopes and dreams of religious freedom at the core of their imagination, mesmerized by the beauty their eyes beheld and pregnant with the possibilities of this new land. As the words of God and Isaiah filled their mental skies, "Behold, I will do a new thing; now it shall spring forth; shall ye not know it. I will even make a way in the wilderness, and rivers in the desert. The beast of the field shall honor the dragons, the owls and me: because I give waters in the wilderness, and streams in the desert, to give drink to my people, my chosen. These people have I formed for myself; they shall show forth my praise." These words floated from God's mouth to the Pilgrims' and Puritans' ears, which was confirmation that this new land was their manifest destiny. Alexis de

Tocqueville noted, "It must never be forgotten that religion gave birth to Anglo-American society. In the United States, religion is therefore mingled with all the habits of the nation and all the feelings of patriotism, whence it derives a peculiar force." President William Howard Taft in a speech celebrating the 250th anniversary of Norwich, Connecticut, in 1909 stated: "We speak with great satisfaction of the fact that our ancestors and I claim New England ancestry, came to this country to establish freedom of religion... Well if you are going to be exact, they came to this country to establish freedom of their religion and not the freedom of anybody else's religion."

President Taft was correct in his assertion that initially the Pilgrims were consumed with their religious freedom. Quite amazing that they could focus on that when their first years in this new land were filled with hunger, sickness, disease, and the mutual mistrust between themselves and the Indians.

**The Mayflower Compact**

The Mayflower Compact was the first agreement set for self-government in America. Forty-one men signed this compact and set up a government for the Plymouth colony. The Mayflower Compact was a far cry from what democracy would eventually become; however, it was a beginning. As Forest Church stated in his book The American Creed:

> The Plymouth Colony was far from being a perfect democracy, and the Massachusetts Bay Colony made no pretense to being one. Though the Pilgrims experimented for a short while with a kind of primitive communism (taking their communitarian script from the Acts of Apostles in the New Testament), the basis for a strict

> hierarchy was present from the beginning. From the covenant theology of Governor William Bradford quickly developed elements suggested of rigid theocracy. The form of government that emerged in Massachusetts was neither egalitarian nor democratic. Nonetheless, at the very outset of our history, the Mayflower Compact established the notion upon which our nation would be founded: governments formed by compact derived their power from the terms set by the governed.

One can easily see that initially in America, there was no clear division between the civic compact and their religious covenant. The Pilgrims were not executing their ideas from human inclination but spiritual ones. These were God's plans for both religious and civic duties. As Forrest Church went on to say, "America is founded on the theological conviction that "God's will and man's weal, are one and the same."

In the early formation of the new American colony came two men who were ministers of God from England. First was the arrival of John Winthrop and later Roger Williams, both true believers, but each had different views on how church and state should be related. John M. Barry in his article "God, Government and Roger Williams' Big Idea" in the Smithsonian describes it this way:

> John Winthrop led 1,000 men, women and children to plant the Massachusetts Bay Colony in 1630. These Puritans were disgusted with what they regarded as corruption in the Church of England and the tyranny of the crown. Seeking simple worship and personal intimacy with God, Puritan ministers were compelled—upon

pain of imprisonment—to wear the surplice and use the Book of Common Prayer, and their congregants were compelled to participate in what they regarded as rote worship. As they set out from England that April, Winthrop reminded them of their purpose, to establish a "city upon a hill" dedicated to God, obeying God's laws and flourishing in God's image as a model for the entire world to see.

Williams, who had developed a reputation for scholarship and loyalty as a clergyman in England, brought his family to the colony a few months later. Winthrop hailed him as "a godly minister," and the Boston church immediately offered him a post, the most significant such position in English America. But Williams declined, spurning the church as insufficiently committed to the proper worship of God. This astonishing charge would put him at odds with the colony's leaders till the day he died.

Williams did not differ with them on any point of theology. They shared the same faith, all worshiping the God of Calvin, seeing God in every facet of life and seeing man's purpose as advancing the kingdom of God. But the colony's leaders, both lay, and clergy, firmly believed that the state must prevent error in religion. They thought that the success of the Massachusetts plantation depended upon it.

Williams believed that preventing error in religion was impossible, for it required people to interpret God's law, and people would inevitably err. He, therefore, concluded that government must remove itself from anything that touched upon human beings' relationship with God. A society built on the principles Williams espoused would lead at best to hypocrisy, because forced worship, he wrote, "stinks in God's nostrils." At worst, such a society would lead to a foul corruption—not of the state, which was already corrupt, but of the church.

The dispute defined for the first time two fault lines that have run through American history ever since. The first, of course, is over the proper relation between government and what man has made of God—the church. The second is over the relation between a free individual and government authority—the shape of liberty.

[...]

In October 1635, the General Court of the Massachusetts Bay Colony banished him, ordering him to leave the colony within six weeks. If he returned, he risked execution.

[...]

Eventually, Williams made his way south to Narragansett Bay and chose a site for a settlement on a cove into which two small rivers emptied. He bought the land from the Narragansett Indians and wrote that "having, of a sense of God's merciful providence unto me in my distress, [I] called the place PROVIDENCE, I desired it might be for a shelter for persons distressed for conscience."

By "conscience" he meant religion. His family and a dozen or so men with their families, many of them followers from Salem, joined him. Few as they were,

Williams soon recognized the need for some form of government; the people of Narragansett had sold the land solely to him; and in all English and colonial precedent, those proprietary rights gave him political control over the settlement. Yet he drafted a political compact for Providence, and in it, he demonstrated that his thinking had taken him into a new world indeed.

He relinquished nearly all his land—to a town common stock—and any exclusive political rights, reserving for himself only a vote equal to others. But the most significant element was what the compact did not say. It did not propose to build a model of God's kingdom on earth, as did Massachusetts. Nor did it even claim to advance God's will, as did the founding documents of every other European settlement in North and South America, whether English, Spanish, Portuguese or French. The compact did not even ask God's blessing. It made no mention of God at all.

[...]

Even the bitterest opponents of Roger Williams recognized in him that combination of charm, confidence, and intensity a later age would call charisma. They did not regard such traits as assets, however, for those characteristics only made the preacher more dangerous in the Massachusetts Bay Colony. With someone like him, they could not compromise.

For his part, Williams was not about to compromise, either, despite his benevolent intelligence and Christian charity. The error, he believed, was not his, and when convinced he was right he backed away from no one.

> So the conflict between Williams and his accusers nearly 400 years ago was inevitable. It was also thick with history, for it concerned both the relationship between church and state and defining the very nature of state power. Its repercussions would be immense and reach into the present.

John Winthrop ascended to the first Governor of the Massachusetts Bay colony. Winthrop was a Puritan lawyer, who was the author of "A Model of Christian Charity." "A Model of Christian Charity" became one of the most influential visions set forth during the 1630s for new, developing colonies' governments and religious frameworks. Winthrop governed from elitist political philosophy and a belief that decisions for the people should rest in the hand of a chosen few. He stood by religious freedoms, but not in the sense of democratic government, which he thought was "the meanest and worst of all forms of government." Winthrop believed that liberty attached to humanity means a license to do as one pleases, which was for him unthinkable. He did not recognize it as a divine attribute; rather, freedom was to be only given "to that which is good, just, and honest." Without strong religious and civil restraints, this was nearly impossible for humanity, which he believed to be, by its very nature, evil.

Mr. Winthrop seemed to have a noble motive, though he appeared to be creating a conservative system, a similar method to that he and the new settlers had just recently departed. However, he recognized the link between liberty and morality, which freedom alone can be and which is a mixed gift. Liberty alone is neutral and depending on how one uses it discloses its value. The truth is not the product of liberty; it is the opposite. Freedom is the result of truth. Simply put, freedom alone is not a virtue. However, truthfulness is a virtue; you must have honesty before liberty reveals its value. As Jesus declared in John 8:32, "And ye shall know the truth, and the truth shall make you free."

For me, the truth is the basis of all freedom; without truth, the so-called liberty is just another prison with a new set of bars. Winthrop embraced an untruth: to assume the very nature of men is always evil, having condemned us all to destruction without giving the transforming power of love a chance. After all, love-transforming energy is the foundation of all Christian belief. However, Winthrop's conservative beliefs began to institutionalize religion, faith, and morality. This Winthrop Christian strand would continue to align with the governmental and economic systems as they started to take shape in America. Reducing humanity to a group whose very nature was to do harm or commit unspeakable evils meant that one would need to protect themselves against this type of sin. This injection of fear helps drive radical individualism and gave birth to a whole litany of evils that America is currently navigating.

There are not many evils that could possibly compare to the many atrocities unleashed during the advent of the Trans-Atlantic slave trade. The new land, the "Promised Land" America, was a place that was created to end the suffering by exporting the promise of freedom cloaked in the fact that it was and is a Christian nation. One must ask did the forefathers as well as the citizens understand the long lasting consequences of getting involved in such a nasty enterprise? The Atlantic slave trade began in 1526, and lasted until 1867 some 12.5 million men, women and children were extracted from their African home, with 10.7 million actually arriving in the Americas. The death toll in this migration was second to none in history.

At the height of the slave trade, there were nearly 100,000 slaves arriving annually. By 1820, there were four Africans for every one European had crossed the Atlantic. However, by 1825, the United States had a quarter of blacks in America. These slaves assisted greatly in production of tobacco, rice, cotton, and indigo, which was the engine that converted America into an economic juggernaut. Some has estimated during the 1800s alone, that it was approximately 6 to 7 million African slaves imported to the US.

I often think about today, what the great nation of Africa could have been, if it had held on to their most precious resource, their people. If we just take a moment to think of the numbers of those who died on this perilous journey. Historians have suggested it could be as many as 2 million. How many more died due to the inhumane working and living conditions. We know slaves suffered from many ailments, including rickets, (a Vitamin D deficiency) tetany, (Vitamin D, calcium and magnesium deficiencies); kwashiorkor (severe protein deficiency), blindness, diarrhea, abdominal swelling, bowed legs; skin legions; whooping cough, convulsions, and respiratory diseases. The slave's early childhood death rate was nearly twice that of whites that were living during that same period. Obviously, the slave trade had an enduring affect on Africa and all other nations that participated in this despicable act.

In the 17th century, the entire concept of what could be categorized as property had begun to shift, further encouraging the slave owners. Thomas Hobbes and John Locke, two premier philosophers, laid the groundwork on social and political issues. Thomas Hobbes was concerned with problems that would stand in the way of human beings living in peace and harmony together; he desired to reduce or eliminate many civil conflicts. John

Locke, on the other hand, in his defining work, Essay Concerning Human Understanding, he tackled the mind and how it goes about acquiring ideas and knowledge itself. For him, it was a synthesis of many different ideas that created knowledge.

These two influential philosophers had similar beliefs when speaking of the human being. They understood that that humanity's natural state was to be free and equal. They went further by stating that for society to thrive, one must sacrifice some of one's individual freedoms. They presented to the world a concept of self: every man has proprietorship over his person. He is responsible for himself, and independently has the right to think and act with an alignment to his own morals and values. If the individual was dependent on another man, he was a child and not free. Man's nature was to rule or to dominate; therefore, men would actively struggle and compete to do so. The government was necessary to ensure fair, equitable play, in the market most of all, but in life also.

Macpherson calls this conception "possessive individualism."

"I own, therefore I am" is the paradigm of possessive individualism, which is a twist on Descartes' "Cogito Ergo Sum," "I think; therefore, I am." A Short History of America Capitalism described it this way:

> Possession and possessing make the man; they also make him free. Such a person cannot conceive of existence apart from possession or the striving after it. Because ownership is the core of self, the person is not himself but what he owns. He is, in a sense, alienated from, without ever having been joined with, himself. He

has senses; his self is problematical. As Tönnies wrote: "... So far as possible he conducts himself toward others as a merchant and toward himself as a hedonist, but dislikes to go about unmasked."

American society from the colonial period onwards was the very opposite of equalitarianism and self-denial in economic affairs. The greatest economic swindle in American history was not the Lincoln Savings & Loan affair, although this is what we have been told repeatedly. Instead, it was the stealing of the Indians' land, which constituted the basis of America's claim to unparalleled economic sufficiency and generosity. Without Indian land, the developments in nearly two centuries of colonial history would have been unthinkable. During the 17th and 18th centuries, the land was the principal means of production in America. Instead of acquiring wealth by retail means such as piracy on the high seas, European Americans stole other people's wealth wholesale.

The very philosophy of individualism facilitated the adoption of slavery. To Locke, as we said earlier, the central tenet of individualism was man's domain over his labor, even to the point of selling it. That right carried no social or moral obligation other than the expectation of buying cheap and selling dear. Enslavement was thus regarded as another expression of an individual's unceasing drive to accumulate property. And because this drive was alleged to belong to the inborn nature of man—it has arisen in the state of nature, Locke tells us—its every expression in civil society seemed only natural.

> American history is the apotheosis of private property. It should not be surprising—nor were the historic Americans surprised—that the principle of property extended to the ownership of human beings. In thoroughly bourgeois society, based on property rights, the pecuniary logic knows no self-limitation. One sells his labor; another buys it; why not, then, permit private appropriation of the laborer himself?"

As we see here, the capitalist system was an animalistic, bloodthirsty, anything-goes, free-market affair, where theft and murder were regular occurrences, and the purveyors of this extreme violence were never held accountable. Even now many have refused to take responsibility for this barbaric assault on humanity, which allowed many to reduce others to subhuman status to support their greed. All of this is facilitating the alignment of a willing government, a supportive Christian church, and a predatory economic system. This tragedy would baffle the mind of even the morally corrupt, and cuts to the core all of us who believe and live by the Golden Rule: "Do unto as others as you would have them do unto you."

Moving hundreds of years forward to the adoption of the U.S. Constitution, the "Founding Fathers" were concerned with the large aggregation of wealth. In the acclaimed Federalist No. 10, James Madison warned of the dangers to democracy of minority factions that subvert popular will, and in particular noted the inevitable presence and risk of an array of factions based on "a landed interest, a manufacturing interest, a mercantile interest, and a moneyed interest." Not long after that, in his 1830s foundational text on the civic spirit of early American, Democracy in America, Alexis de Tocqueville noted:

The political parties, which I style great, are those who cling to principles more than to their consequences; in general, and not to special cases; to ideas, and not to men. A nobler character usually distinguishes these parties, by more generous passions, more genuine convictions, and more bold and open conduct than the others. In them private interest, which always plays the chief part in political passions, is more studiously veiled under the pretext of the public good; and it may even be sometimes concealed from the eyes of the very persons whom it excites and impels.

Minor parties are, on the other hand, generally deficient in political faith. As they are not sustained or dignified by a lofty purpose, they ostensibly display the egotism of their character in their actions. They glow with a factitious zeal; their language is vehement, but their conduct is timid and irresolute. The means they employ are as wretched as the end at which they aim. Hence it arises that when a calm state of things succeeds a violent revolution, the leaders of society seem suddenly to disappear, and the powers of the human mind to lie concealed. Society is convulsed by great parties, by minor ones it is agitated; it is torn by the former, by the latter it is degraded; and if these sometimes save it by a salutary perturbation, those invariably disturb it to no good end.

America has already lost the great parties, which once divided the nation; and if her happiness is considerably increased, her morality has suffered by their extinction. When the War of Independence was terminated, and

> the foundations of the new Government were to be laid down, the nation was divided between two opinions—two opinions which are as old as the world, and which are perpetually to be met with under all the forms and all the names which have ever obtained in free communities—the one tending to limit, the other to extend indefinitely, the power of the people. The conflict of these two opinions never assumed that degree of violence in America which it has frequently displayed elsewhere. Both parties of the Americans were, in fact, agreed upon the essential points; and neither of them had to destroy a traditional constitution, or to overthrow the structure of society, to ensure its triumph. In neither of them, consequently, were a great number of private interests affected by success or by defeat; but moral principles of a high order, such as the love of equality and independence, were concerned in the struggle, and they sufficed to kindle violent passions.

This argument has continued until today and will proceed into the future. The danger here lies in our inability to sever ties between faith, politics, and the capitalist economic system. Our faith should permeate every aspect of our being. However, it should not infringe on the rights of others within the process, to allow this infringement would unjustly imprison those minorities who chose a separate path. Christ's message was one of love and hopes to persuade one to reconsider their chosen path, but not to legislate morality as they attempted to do in the days of Moses. A free people have an individual God-given right to choose. Sure, any society needs laws. However, these laws are to be aligned with the unalienable rights, to protect against the infringement of others upon another's rights, and to secure the individual's right of the pursuit of happiness. Neither should an economic system seek to dominate the global community as if it is the answer to the world problems; it is a system, therefore neutral, and it rises and falls to the moral capacity of its participants. So, to allow a system that has been manipulated to benefit the entrenched few, to be exported, would be approving the further exploitation of the global community. Because, when we export Democracy, we also ship Christianity, capitalism, and all of its animalistic predatory practices.

> "What constitutes an American? Not color nor race nor religion. Not the pedigree of his family or the place of his birth. The coincidence of his citizenship, neither his social status, nor his bank account, neither his trade, nor his profession, an American is one who loves justice and believes in the dignity of man. An American is one who will fight for his freedom and that of his neighbor. An American is one who will sacrifice property, ease and security in order that he and his children may retain the rights of free men. An American is one in whose heart is engraved the immortal second sentence of the Declaration of Independence."
>
> —Harold Ickes

> "Certainly the most destructive vice if you like, that a person can have—more than pride, which is supposedly the number one of the cardinal sins—is self-pity. Self-pity is the worst possible emotion anyone can have, and the most destructive. It is, to slightly paraphrase what Wilde said about hatred, and I think actually hatred's a subset of self-pity and not the other way around—"It destroys everything around it, except itself. Self-pity will

destroy relationships, it'll destroy anything that's good, and it will fulfill all the prophecies it makes and leave only itself. And it's so simple to imagine that one is hard done by, and that things are unfair, and that one is under-appreciated, and that if only one had had a chance at this, only one had had a chance at that, things would have gone better, you would be happier if only this, that one is unlucky. All those things, and some of them may well even be true. But, to pity oneself as a result of them is to do oneself an enormous disservice. I think it's one of the things we find unattractive about the American culture, a culture which I find mostly, extremely attractive, and I like Americans and I love being in America. But, just occasionally there will be some example of the absolutely ravening self-pity that they are capable of, and you see it in their talk shows. It's an appalling spectacle, and it's so self-destructive. I almost once wanted to publish a self-help book saying "How To Be Happy by Stephen Fry: Guaranteed success." And people buy this huge book and it's all blank pages, and the first page would just say—' Stop Feeling Sorry For Yourself—and you will be happy '. Use the rest of the book to write down your interesting thoughts and drawings, and that's what the book would be, and it would be true. And it sounds like "Oh, that's so simple," because it's not simple to stop feeling sorry for yourself, it's bloody hard. Because we do feel sorry for ourselves, it's what Genesis is all about."

—Stephen Fry

We as a nation must continue to fight for those things that are aligned with our Constitution, our Bill of Rights, and our ideas.

Yes, this must be fought for on local, state, and national levels. However, each individual must work to ensure that they are living up to the vision, which is America. We cannot sit on the sidelines of our own existence. We must be active in our personal development, to be the example of what was intended. We cannot embrace this degenerate culture that lifts our greatest sin to a position of noteworthiness. We cannot export our mistakes and bad ideas that have caused America great pain. What we can export is the good, and the stories of how we defeated and overcame these bad ideas; the belief in the equality of all men and the individual's God-given right to the pursuit of happiness. Each of these God -given rights does not just depend on the enforcement of the judicial system, but requires each of us to practice them daily in our individual lives.

# IGNORANCE IS BLISS

"Ignorance is bliss," that's my motto. The less you know the better, whatever the subject is. I look around and I see people desperate to learn, people who work so hard to have the best education, and little do they know that what they've spent their whole lives trying to accomplish is what will lead to their utter misery. Don't be fooled! Education is nothing but a conspiracy created by those who are secretly controlling the world. Whoever they are. Schools are organizations formed to brainwash children and provide them with destructive data and knowledge. Teachers are merely agents working to demolish our future. They're trying to eradicate ignorance and fill our minds with plenty of information to have us dazed and confused while they control the world. Ignorance is bliss, and genius, is hell.

When you pass by a hobo who's standing in the middle of the street, smiling at people's faces with a handful of coins clutched in his palms, and you ask yourself why he's so happy? Do you think it's because they're educated and full of knowledge? No. It's because their life is lavished with treasured ignorance. I envy these people. I despise my parents for forcing me to attend school and learn what I now try so hard to erase from my mind. I also pity them for dying believing that intelligence is the key to a fruitful life. Look at Albert Einstein, Isaac Newton and Thomas Edison. Look what intelligence got them to, only death. Can you name any influential ignorant people that have ended up like those people did? I don't think so.

We must make it our number one priority to fight these knowledge-spreading institutions and make this world a better place for our children. A place full of ignorance, inexperience and what's the first step you take in order to defeat your enemy? Destroy their most powerful weapon. Books. Books are the bringer of knowledge. Books carry the words of those who plot to rid the world of ignorance. And they're everywhere. All around you, you will see this horrible weapon disguising itself as a useful tool when in fact it destroys lives. By providing a massive effort into bringing awareness to this, we will be able to raise enough money to fund what I call, "The War on Books" or "The War on Knowledge". Don't listen to schemers like Ray Bradbury (Author of 'Fahrenheit 451') who try to make you believe that books are treasures that should be read and protected. Books should be thrown away, burned, destroyed! History, Science, Philosophy, Math, Economics, Arts; they're all poisonous subjects created by the conspirators to destroy your brain and lead you in the wrong direction. Don't be fooled!

"To change the world, you must first start with yourself. So if you want to play a major role in the War on Knowledge, you need to begin locally. The first step you should take is to get rid of any books, especially Encyclopedias, or any source of knowledge. If you're forced by your parents to attend a school then I advise you to

> stand up to them and drop out immediately. Don't talk to teachers and cover your ears every time they start to speak. Then, start gathering a few friends and form an assembly, and start convincing other people to join in. But be vigilant and keep your group underground for the time being. Try your best to abolish books and sabotage schools. Make sure you don't have any moles in your brotherhood; teachers shouldn't be underestimated. The bigger and stronger you grow, the more enemies you will have. Keep doing this and step-by-step many groups will flourish into one huge crowd, and then, only then, will the "Ignorant Revolution" truly begin. And history will remember our names."
>
> —Youssef Shaalan

The above article is of course a spoof, but though it sounds outrageous, a great deal of it we are currently witnessing. The American society is becoming less and less interested in knowledge and thought. Despite the fact that we are living in the Information Age, we have become very isolated in our thinking, if we choose to think at all. As things become readily available in our society, and the country drifts more into the mentality of not recognizing patience as a virtue, we must have things now, and thoughtful study and reflection become a chore that no one seems to be interested in practicing anymore. In the Alan Bloom book, The Closing of the American Mind, he tackles this phenomenon by disclosing what he saw as the dumbing down of America. Jacob Hamburger, a writer for The Point magazine, put it this way:

> "For Bloom, then, the university was the most important institution of American democracy. Taking

Plato at his word, he believed that the people who rule it best express the character of a society. It followed that colleges and universities, the training ground for America's elites, had the task of ensuring that the country's leaders embodied the basic principles of its political regime. As long as they practiced genuine liberal education, Bloom believed these institutions could continue to produce "statesmen" trained in the responsible exercise of democratic freedom. Though he praised democracy in principle, he believed it an "intellectual wasteland," indifferent or even hostile to serious thinking. For a democracy to thrive, talented youngsters had to be exposed to a philosophical education that allowed them to transcend the "bourgeois vulgarity" of their surroundings, and to devote themselves to something other than mere self-advancement. If American society could not ensure this, it risked descending into rule by elites who were no better than the uneducated mob, and for this reason perhaps far more dangerous (such was apparently his assessment of the graduates of MBA programs). As a result, Bloom believed that a "crisis of liberal education" would amount to nothing less than "the crisis of our civilization."

Bloom recognized, however, that his ideal picture of democratic education required a delicate social balance. Only under certain conditions will ordinary Americans put their trust in a liberally educated elite. A cultural conservative, Bloom saw America's strong moral traditions as the key to its success in maintaining such a balance. Unlike Western Europe, where the collapse of traditional cultures had led to the crises of the 1930s,

America had succeeded for much of its history in preserving an authentic attachment to both Judeo-Christian and civil religions. He wrote nostalgically of his forebears:

"My grandparents were ignorant people by our standards, and my grandfather held only lowly jobs. But their home was spiritually rich because all the things done in it, not only what was specifically ritual, found their origin in the Bible's commandments. … Their simple faith and practices linked them to great scholars and thinkers who dealt with the same material. … There was a respect for real learning, because it had a felt connection with their lives."

For Bloom, the vitality of tradition, whether grounded in the Bible or the Constitution, meant that people of earlier times not only respected the authority of those with knowledge, but could also become educated themselves. Students raised in these traditions went to college full of deeply held "prejudices," which Bloom counterintuitively saw as crucial for an authentic education. "One has to have the experience of really believing," he wrote, "before one can have the thrill of liberation." And the lesson Bloom drew for the present moment was the same: once the university falls, democracy itself is soon to follow. The "open-minded" relativism and fervent egalitarianism of his students convinced him that, after twenty years, this "crisis of our civilization" was far from over.

For Bloom, the only solution to the impending collapse of democracy was for elite universities to unilaterally withdraw from society, returning to a traditional humanities curriculum. Earlier in his life, he had thought that America was gradually becoming a more enlightened nation. The prestigious universities were by far the finest source of intellectual cultivation American democracy had to offer, but they could count on other institutions to assist them in achieving a sort of general progress. In Closing, he expressed a radically different view. "Never did I think that the university was properly ministerial to the society around it," he wrote towards the end of the book.

In order to survive in dark times, Bloom called for the university to renounce its responsibility to society. His ultimate aspiration was for "a society that tolerates and supports an eternal childhood for some," in the hopes that this "playfulness can in turn be a blessing to society." In other words, to use a term he likely never heard of, Bloom longed to re-establish the university as a "safe space" for authentic philosophical learning. The greater the separation between the elite campus and the world around it, the better the chances for democracy's survival.

The great irony is that Bloom's emphatically elitist book helped spark a decades-long wave of conservative polemics against the academic elite. In 1988, the University of Michigan attempted to introduce "speech codes" regulating communication between students; the same year, Stanford revised its mandatory course in "Western Civilization" in response to student demands for more diverse authors. Sharing Bloom's bitterness towards the former student radicals, conservatives cited these trends as evidence that the Sixties had indeed "closed the minds" of elite college students. Closing's success created a new niche for conservative intellectuals like Roger Kimball and Dinesh D'Souza, who followed Bloom with their own books peering into college campuses with scornful delight. President George H. W. Bush used a 1991 commencement speech to warn of the dangers of "political correctness." For many secular conservatives, these attacks on academia helped forge common ground with the traditionalist and religious populism of the Reagan coalition. College students and professors became a common enemy of the right, a "liberal elite" to blame for America's cultural decline.

After a period of relative quiet, "political correctness" returned to the center of nationwide polemics around two years ago. The terms of the debate had changed slightly. With "trigger warnings" and "safe spaces," campus egalitarianism adopted an emotional vocabulary relatively absent from the discourse of the Eighties and Nineties, one that sought to highlight the traumatic experiences of marginalized students. And centrist liberals began to take up the "anti-PC" role once occupied predominantly by conservatives. The main substance of the conversation over diversity at elite institutions, however, remains largely the same as in Bloom's day. Around the time Greg Lukianoff and Jonathan Haidt's Atlantic article "The Coddling of the American Mind" was making its rounds in the fall of 2015, it might have been reasonable to roll one's eyes at this regurgitation of old polemics. But soon after, as the 2016 presidential cam-

> paign began, such debates began to take on a renewed political significance.
>
> For Donald Trump, "political correctness" has long referred to whatever he does not like at any given moment. But Breitbart and the other alt-right sites his presidency has brought into the daylight have turned outrage over "social justice warriors" into the clarion call of a new political community. The idea that there is an epidemic of "political correctness" allows the new American right to perform a dangerous sleight of hand. When the president denounces "elites" or dismisses criticism as "politically correct," he invokes the most extreme images from American college campuses, like the video of the "shrieking girl" at Yale, which the alt right has circulated with glee. The political danger is patent. Opposition to the cruelest of Trump's proposals is, in this hijacked discourse, not a sensible moral position but a symptom of a decadent liberal elitism."

Nihilism is the belief that traditional morals, ideas, beliefs, etc., have no value; a viewpoint that traditional values and beliefs are unfounded and that existence is senseless and useless; a doctrine that denies any objective ground of truth and especially of moral truths. Relativism is the belief that different things are true, right, etc., for different people or at different times; a theory that knowledge is about the limited nature of the mind and the conditions of knowing; a view that ethical truths depend on the individuals and groups holding them.

Nihilism and relativism have joined forces to wreak havoc throughout our American society. They have attempted to destroy our foundational truths, with a watered-down variable value system, that changes depending on the individuals involved in the discussion. The truth is so complicated to nail down these days, not because it is hiding, but because people have negotiated the truth from these relative perspectives. There is truly one truth; there are not multiple truths, however, talk to most Americans today and they will say, you have your truth, and I have mine. They fail to see that a small change in how we think will affect how we speak, and the change in how an individual thinks and speaks changes how one will behave. In our ignorance we reinforce degenerate culture and endorse it as the norm, exposing future generations to all the fruit that adopting willful ignorance would bring.

> "Where there is no vision, the people perish: but he that keepeth the law, happy is he."
>
> —Proverbs 29:18

> "My people are destroyed for lack of knowledge. Because you have rejected knowledge, I also will reject you from being my priest. Since you have forgotten the law of your God, I also will forget your children."
>
> —Hosea 4:6

These two scriptures from the Bible are identifying how God judges ignorance. It appears that there are no passes given to those who remain ignorant; inevitably you cannot be an effective representative of His without a thirst for knowledge. He goes on to say in Hosea 4:6 that since you have forgotten the law of your God, I will forget your children. In Proverbs 29:18 there is a linkage between vision and his law, and in Hosea, it is a linkage between knowledge and law. I believe this merely points to remembering and keeping his law as the foundation of vision and knowledge, and apart from that, our future becomes bleak, and we are doomed to fail. These two statements were indeed a warning to the people who lived during that period, and I believe the same is a warning to us today. I believe that God's law which was put forth in the Bible and echoed in the Declaration of Independence must undergird any systems used for humanity.

"We hold these truths to be self-evident, that all men are created equal, that they are endowed by their Creator with certain unalienable Rights, that among these are Life, Liberty and the Pursuit of Happiness."

The Declaration of Independence gives the thesis of America's thoughts and ultimate goals; this also provided a framework for all American institutions and policies, both domestic and foreign. Now, for the citizens of America to support these institutions, policies, both home and abroad, we must live by a higher moral code, free from absolute selfishness but according to God's law, which is to "do unto others as you would have them to do unto you." Within that statement is displayed that our well-being ultimately depends on how we treat others. Therefore, within systems, our institutions, policies, and laws must govern themselves with the Declaration of Independence and the participants or citizens must govern their actions by the "Golden Rule," which are both in alignment with God's law.

> "Nothing in the world is more dangerous than sincere ignorance and conscientious stupidity."
>
> —Martin Luther King Jr.

> "Ignorance, the root and stem of all evil."
>
> —Plato

However, today the level of inequality is unprecedented. 99% of the world's wealth is held by 1% of its population; this has had a corrosive effect on democracy. The American Dream is primarily based on the mobility of the middle class, and when the middle class is squeezed, and the income divide continues to increase, it has meant throughout history that some catastrophic problems lay ahead. A concentration of wealth yields to a centralization of power, especially in the political climate we have today, this is out of line with a democracy. In a democracy, public opinion typically influences some public policies. Therefore, the government carries out policy based on public opinion, which is what a democratic society is intended to be. The wealthy, privileged, and powerful sectors have never liked or wanted democracy only because it takes power away from them and gives it to the people.

So as the cost of elections dramatically increases, it forces the political parties into the pockets of the wealthy and major corporations. This political power quickly translates into the legislative influence that increases the concentration of wealth by creating more favorable fiscal policies, like tax policy, deregulation, rules of corporate governance, and many other political measures designed to increase the concentration of wealth and power. Eventually, this creates a vicious cycle where wealth and power are centralized and growing through legislative influence, which mutes the voices of the population, which in turn cripples democracy as a whole.

This type of manipulation of democracy is so traditional that Adam Smith described it in 1776. In his book Wealth of Nations, in England, the principal architects of policy are the people who run the society. In his day, merchants and manufacturers ensured that their interests were cared for no matter how catastrophic it may have been for the people of England. Today it is not merchants and manufacturers but financial institutions, and multi-national corporations, the people Adam Smith called the "Masters of Mankind," who follow the vile maxim, "all for ourselves and nothing for anyone else."

> "There is a cult of ignorance in the United States, and there has always been. The strain of anti-intellectualism has been a constant thread winding its way through our political and cultural life, nurtured by the false notion that democracy means that 'my ignorance is just as good as your knowledge."
>
> —Isaac Asimov

In the Requiem for the American Dream documentary, Noam Chomsky, the linguist, cognitive scientist, historian, social critic, and political activist speaks, about the ten principles of concentrating wealth and power.

The first is the reduction of democracy. Throughout history, we have seen the pressures within democracy itself where the people are pushing from below for more freedom and access and the powers above want more wealth, power, control, and domination. Again, this is not new; this has been a part of the American tapestry from the beginning. James Madison was one of the principal architects of our Constitution and a believer in our democracy. He believed that our democracy should be designed where the wealthy would be protected and have control over the system. Madison believed that the wealthy were more responsible men and should be entrusted with power. The structure of the Constitution gave extreme power to the Senate—during that time the Senate was not elected but a group of wealthy men which Madison thought would be considerate of property owners and their rights. In the debates of the Constitutional Convention, Madison argued that the goal of society was "to protect the minority of the opulent against the majority." He made an argument to bolster his position: he supposed that if the poor majority voted to take all the land from the wealthy landowners, that would be unjust, and therefore the Constitutional system needed to be set up to prevent this from occurring by reducing democracy.

If we go back to the first significant book on politics, which was Aristotle's Politics, he addressed democracy and saw it as an excellent governmental system, but he saw some flaws similar to what Madison revealed. However, his solution to the problem was much different from Madison's answer. Aristotle believed the way to confront the issue was to reduce inequality and democracy would be fine. These two systems of thinking have been in an ongoing battle in America from the beginning, and even today.

# INEQUALITY

Inequality is the condition of being unequal, social or economic disparity, unequal opportunity or treatment or relative inadequacy in natural endowments—a widening gap in intellect, talents, healthcare, education, wealth, and access. Inequality is largely based on the mobility of the middle class and therefore a must in a thriving democracy. Without the middle class, a democracy is at grave risk. In Aristotle's book Politics he noted:

> The best constitution is one controlled by a numerous middle class, which stands between the rich and the poor. For those who possess the goods of fortune in moderation find it "easiest to obey the rule of reason" (Politics IV.11.1295b4–6). They are accordingly less apt than the rich or poor to act unjustly toward their fellow citizens. A constitution based on the middle class is the mean between the extremes of oligarchy (rule by the rich) and democracy (rule by the poor). "That the middle [constitution] is best is evident, for it is the freest from faction: where the middle class is numerous, there least occur factions and divisions among citizens" (IV.11.1296a7–9). The middle constitution is therefore both more stable and more just than oligarchy and democracy.

Aristotle also noted:

> The best political community is formed by citizens of the middle class, and that those states are likely to be

> well-administered in which the middle class is larger, and stronger if possible than both the other classes … for the addition of the middle class turns the scale, and prevents either of the extremes from being dominant.

The richest, most privileged, and most powerful sectors have never wanted a Democracy, it takes power away from them and gives it to the people. A concentration of wealth yields to a concentration of power. Adam Smith spoke of this in the wealth of nations … He noted: the principal architects ensure their interest is provided for; they lived by the vile maxim, "all for ourselves and nothing for anyone else." Throughout history and even today they pursue policies that benefit them and no one else. James Madison, one of the authors of the Constitution, believed the rich were better men than others because they were more responsible. The structure of the Constitution gave extreme power to the Senate, which wasn't elected back then, but was appointed, and all Senators were wealthy white men. At the Constitutional Convention debates, Madison argued that the goal is to ensure that they protect the opulent minority from the poverty-stricken majority and wanted to limit democracy. He feared that if the majority had too much political power they could vote away the lands and riches of the wealthy. Madison was more interested in having the appearance of a democracy with limited power to the poor, and more, but still limited power to the middle class, and the lion's share to the wealthy.

The Stanford Center on Poverty & Inequality provided "20 Facts About U.S. Inequality That Everyone Should Know:

**1. Wage Inequality**

Over the last 30 years, wage inequality in the United States has increased substantially, with the overall level of inequality now approaching the extreme level that prevailed prior to the Great Depression. This general characterization of the inequality trend oversimplifies, though, the actual pattern of change. The chart below shows that the trend at the top of the income distribution (the "upper tail") is not exactly the same as the trend at the bottom of the distribution (the "lower tail"). "Lower-tail" inequality is measured here by taking the ratio of wages at the middle of the income distribution (i.e., the 50th percentile) to those near the bottom of the distribution (i.e., the 10th percentile); "upper-tail" inequality is measured by taking the ratio of wages near the top of the distribution (i.e., the 90th percentile) to those at the middle of the distribution (i.e., the 50th percentile of workers). We find that lower-tail inequality rose sharply in the 1980s and contracted somewhat thereafter, while upper-tail inequality has increased steadily since 1980.

**Men's wage inequality**

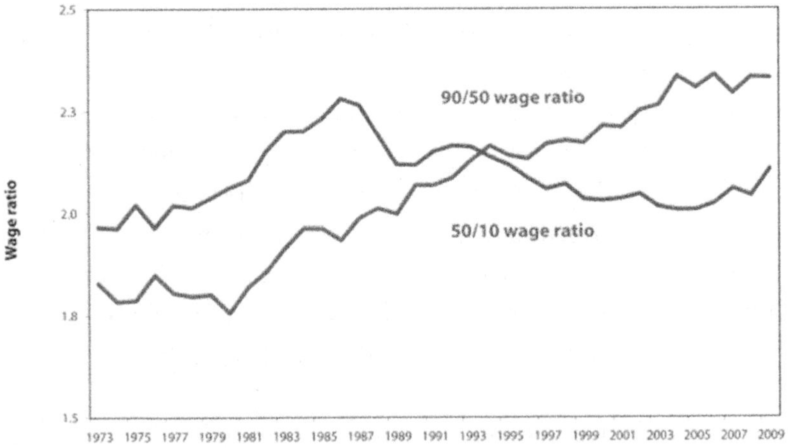


Source: Economic Policy Institute, 2011. "Upper Tail" inequality growing steadily: Men's wage inequality, 1973-2009. Washington, D.C.: Economic Policy Institute. May 11, 2011. <http://www.stateofworkingamerica.org/charts/view/192>.

## 2. CEO pay

Recent decades have seen a clear increase in the difference between CEO compensation and that of the average worker in manufacturing or "production." CEOs in 1965 made 24 times more than the average production worker, whereas in 2009 they made 185 times more. This chart shows how this ratio between the compensation of CEOs and production workers took off in the 1980s. U.S. CEO pays in relation to the average production worker's compensation.

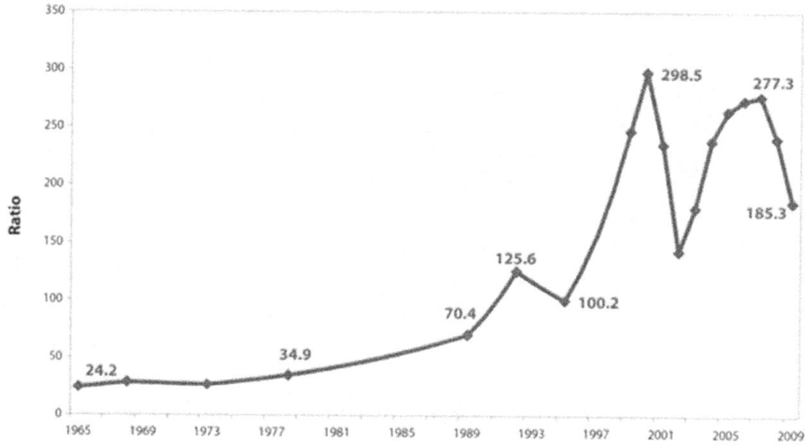


Source: Economic Policy Institute. 2011. More compensation heading to the very top: Ratio of average CEO total direct compensation to average production worker compensation, 1965-2009. Washington, D.C.: Economic Policy Institute. May 16, 2011. <http://www.stateofworkingamerica.org/charts/view/17>.

## 3. Homelessness.

There are 750,000 Americans who are homeless on any given night, with one in five of them considered chronically homeless. The ranks of the sheltered homeless include disproportionate numbers of males, blacks, middle-aged people (i.e., ages 31-50), veterans, and disabled.

**Who is Homeless?**

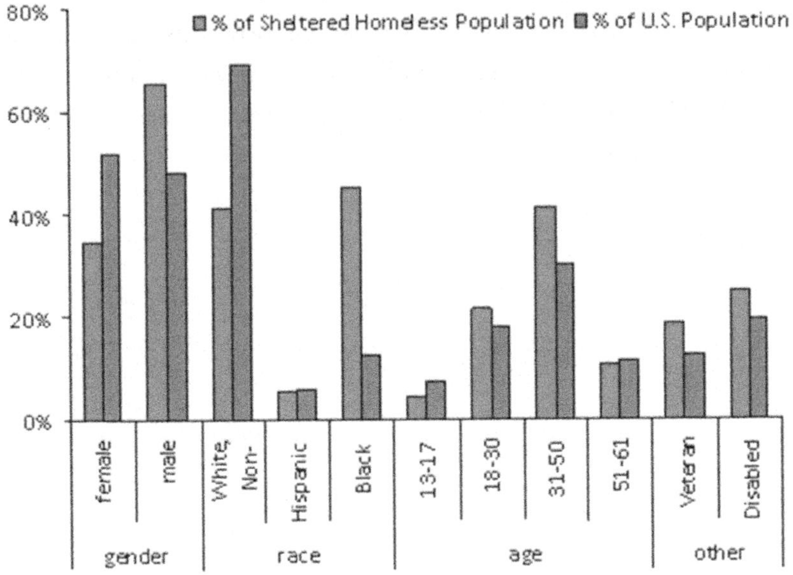


Source: U.S. Department of Housing and Urban Development. 2007. The Annual Homeless Assessment Report to Congress. See http://www.huduser.org/Publications/pdf/ahar.pdf.

**4. Education Wage Premium**

Only college graduates have experienced growth in median weekly earnings since 1979 (in real terms). High school dropouts have, by contrast, seen their real median weekly earnings decline by about 22 percent.

**Median weekly earnings of full-time workers (workers 25 years old & older, 2006 dollars)**

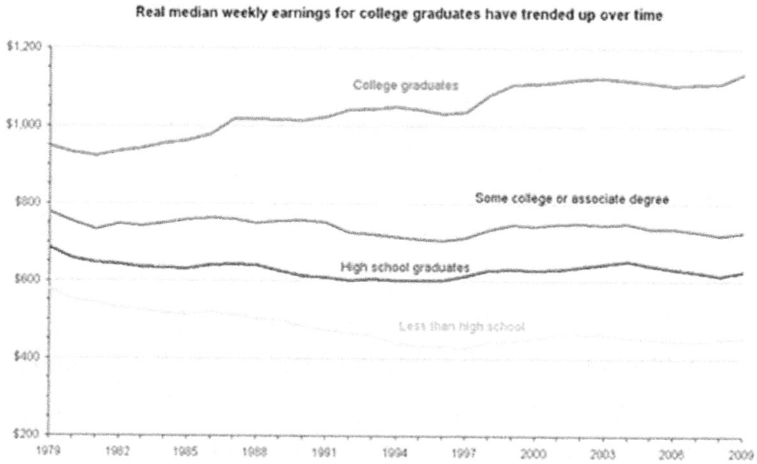


Source: Bureau of Labor Statistics, Charting the U.S. Labor Market in 2006; see http://www.bls.gov/cps/labor2006/home.htm. Updated to 2009 by Steve Hipple of the Bureau of Labor Statistics; see http://economix.blogs.nytimes.com/2010/05/17/the-value-of-college-2/

**5. Gender Pay Gaps**

Throughout much of the 20th century, the average woman earned about 60% of what the average man earned. Starting in the late 1970s, there was a substantial increase in women's relative earnings, with women coming to earn about 80% of what men earned. This historic rise plateaued in 2005 and, since then, the pay gap has remained roughly unchanged.

**Women's earnings as a percent of men's (full-time wage and salary workers, annual averages)**

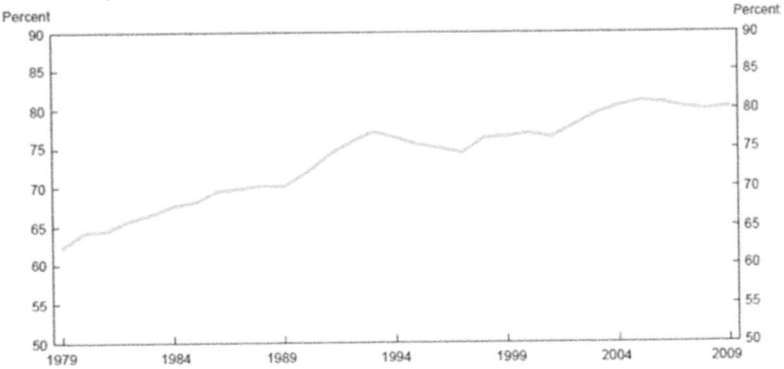


Source: U.S. Department of Labor, Bureau of Labor Statistics. 2010. Highlights of Women's Earnings in 2009. Report 1017. See http://www.bls.gov/cps/cpswom2009.pdf.

## 6. Occupational Sex Segregation

Women and men tend to work in very different occupations. and Overall "men's jobs" are better paid than "women's jobs."

**Gendered occupations and unequal rewards**

Source: U.S. Department of Labor, Bureau of Labor Statistics. 2009. Highlights of Women's Earnings in 2008. Report 1017. See http://www.bls.gov/cps/cpswom2008.pdf.

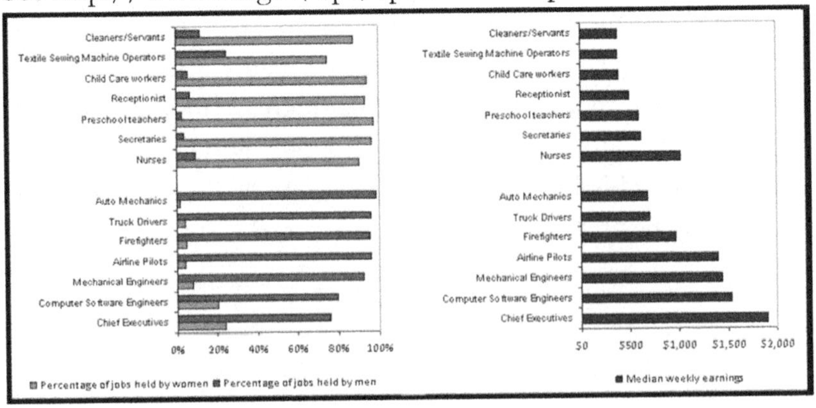

## 7. Racial Gaps in Education

High-school dropout rates are least among whites and highest among Hispanics, while college enrollment rates are least among blacks and highest among whites. The high-school dropout rate has grown more similar among these three groups, while the college enrollment rate has grown more sharply different.

**High school dropout percentage (among persons 16-24 years old) and college enrollment percentage (among high school graduates)**

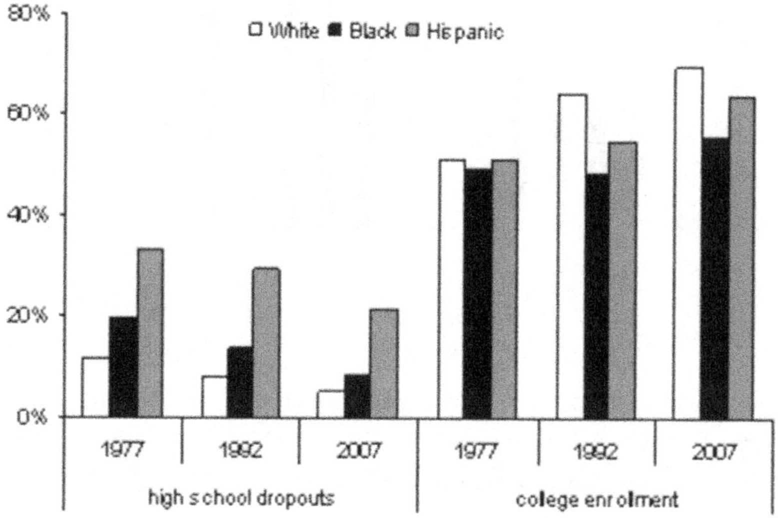


Source: The Digest of Education Statistics 2008, National Center for Education Statistics.

## 8. Racial Discrimination

Racial discrimination continues to be in the labor market. An experiment carried out in Chicago and Boston during 2001 and

2002 shows that resumes with "white-sounding" names, whether male or female, were much more likely to result in call backs for interviews than were those with "black-sounding" names (even though the resumes were otherwise identical).

**Interview callback rate for women with "white" names and "black" names.**

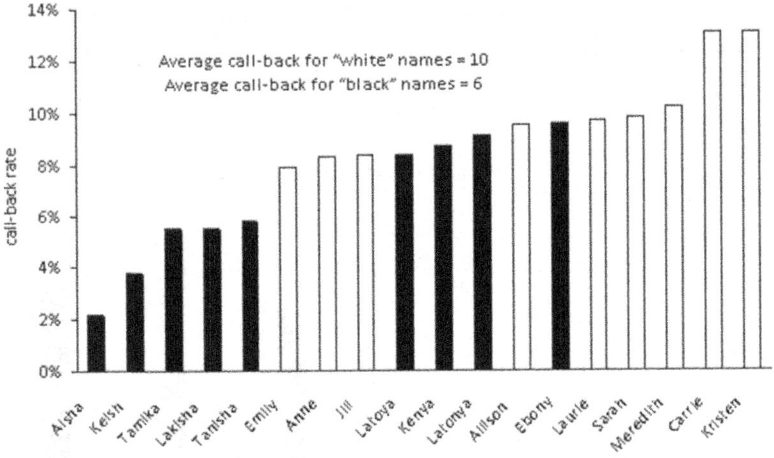


Source: Bertrand, Marianne and Sendhil Mullainathan. 2004. "Are Emily and Greg More Employable than Lakisha and Jamal?" American Economic Review 94(4): 991-1013.

**9. Child Poverty**

In the United States, 21 percent of all children are in poverty, a poverty rate higher than what prevails in virtually all other rich nations.

**Relative Poverty Rates in Forty Nations in the Mid-to-Late 2000s**

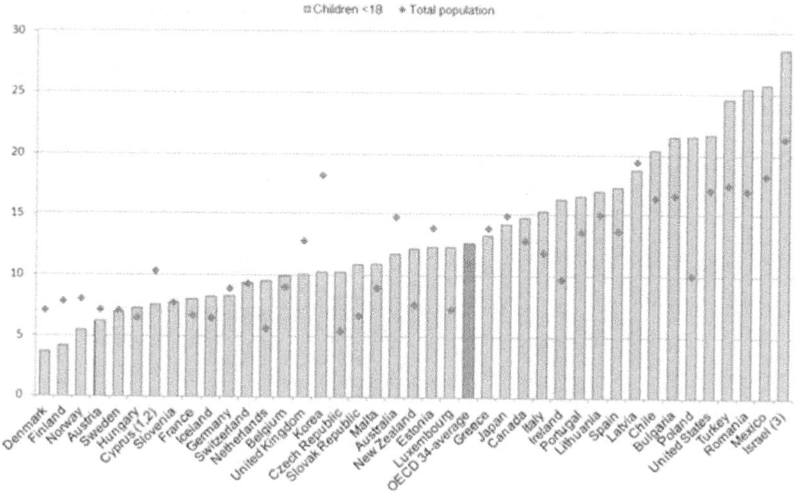


Source: OECD Income Distribution questionnaire, February 2011. Data refer to 2008 for Germany, Israel, Italy, Korea, Mexico, Netherlands, New Zealand, Norway, Sweden and the United States; 2007 for Canada, Denmark and Hungary; 2006 for Chile, Estonia, Japan and Slovenia; 2005 for France, Ireland, Switzerland and the United Kingdom; 2004 for Australia, Austria, Belgium, Czech Republic, Finland, Greece, Iceland, Luxembourg, Poland, Portugal, the Slovak Republic, Spain and Turkey.

## 10. Residential Segregation

We all know that the rich in the United States tend not to live in the same neighborhoods as the poor. But did you know that such residential segregation is on the rise? The graph below reveals that, between 1970 and 2000, there has been a sizable increase in segregation. We show this result by measuring (a) how likely it is for households in the top fifth of the income distribution to live with households not in the top fifth (in 1970 and 2000), and (b) how likely it is for households in the bottom fifth of the income distribution to live with households not in the bottom fifth (again in 1970 and 2000).

**Class-based segregation**

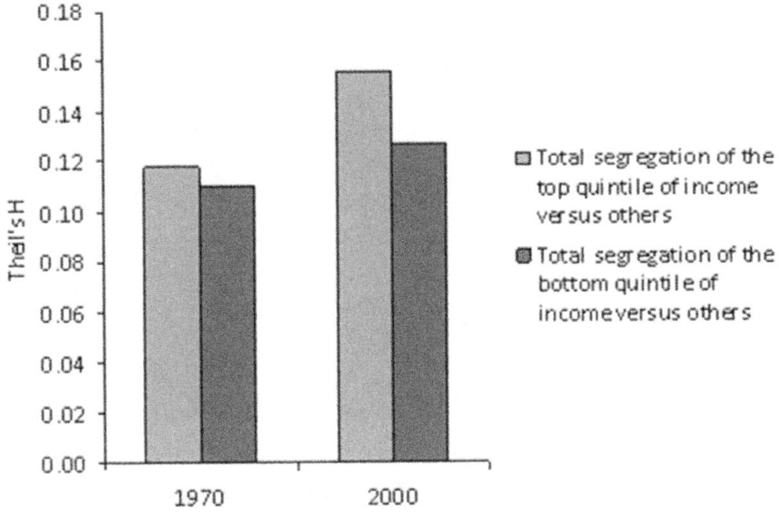


Source: Claude S. Fischer, Gretchen Stockmayer, Jon Stiles, Michael Hout. 2004. "Distinguishing the Geographic Levels and Social Dimensions of U.S. Metropolitan Segregation, 1960-2000." Demography 41(1): 37-59.

**11. Health insurance**

In 2007, 8.1 million children under 18 years old were without health insurance. Children in poverty and Hispanic children were more likely to be uninsured.

**Uninsured Children by Poverty Status, Age, and Race and Hispanic Origin (percent)**

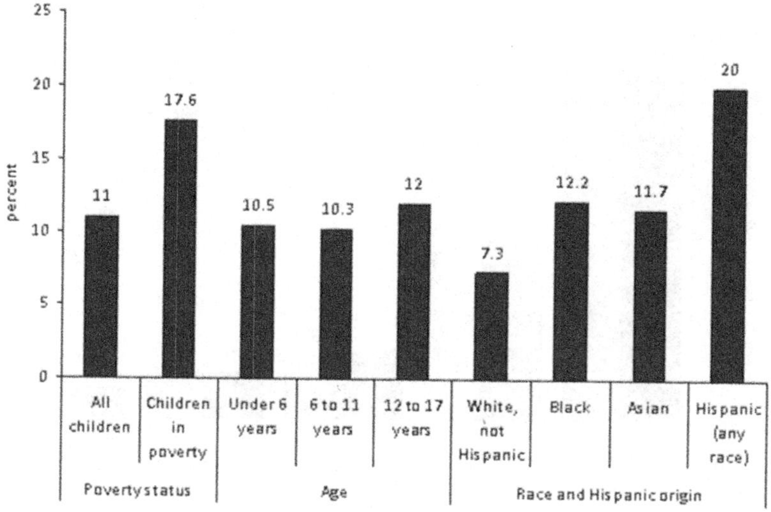


Source: U.S. Census Bureau, Current Population Reports. 2008. Income, Poverty, and Health Insurance Coverage in the United States: 2007. See http://www.census.gov/prod/2008pubs/p60-235.pdf.

## 12. Intra-generational Income Mobility

Intra-generational income mobility refers to the rate at which a person moves to a higher or lower income level during her or his work career. More than half of those individuals in the bottom income quintile in 1994 remained there 10 years later, and less than 4 percent reached the top quintile.

**Relative Mobility Out of the Bottom Income Quintile (individuals age 25 to 44)**

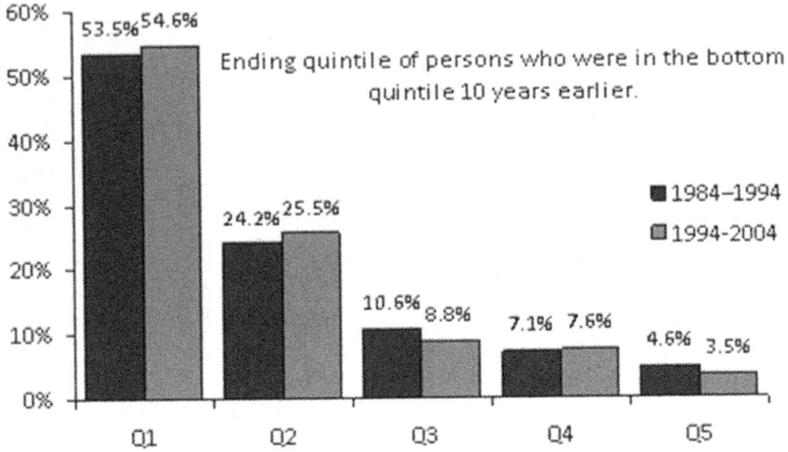


Source: Gregory Acs and Seth Zimmerman. 2008. U.S. Intragenerational Economic Mobility From 1984 to 2004. The Urban Institute. See http://www.urban.org/UploadedPDF/1001226_intragenerational_economic_mobi....

**13. Bad Jobs**

"Bad jobs" are typically considered those that pay low wages and do not include access to health insurance and pension benefits. As shown here, about 10% of full-time workers are in low-wage jobs, about 30% don't have health insurance, and about 40% don't have pensions. The graph also shows that the likelihood of being in a bad job is much worse for part-time workers, for on-call and day laborers, and for those working for temporary help agencies.

**Employment relations and job characteristics**

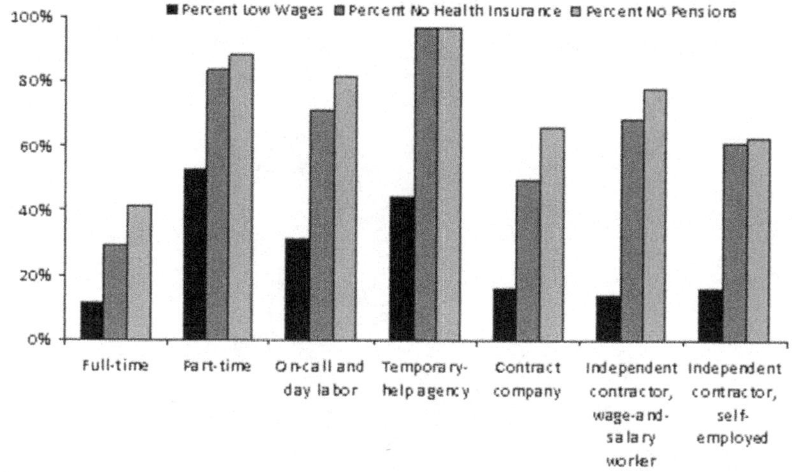


Source: Arne L. Kalleberg, Barbara F. Reskin, Ken Hudson. 2000. "Bad Jobs in America: Standard and Nonstandard Employment Relations and Job Quality in the United States." American Sociological Review 65(2): 256-278.

**14. Discouraged Workers.**

Discouraged workers are persons not currently looking for work because they believe that there are no jobs available for them. The number of discouraged workers in the U.S. increased sharply during the current recession, rising to 717,000 in the first quarter of 2009, a 70-percent increase from the first quarter of 2008. Relative to their share of the labor force, young people, blacks, and, to a lesser extent, Hispanics and men were over-represented among discouraged workers.

**Unemployed and marginally attached workers in first quarter of 2009 (as share of the civilian population)**

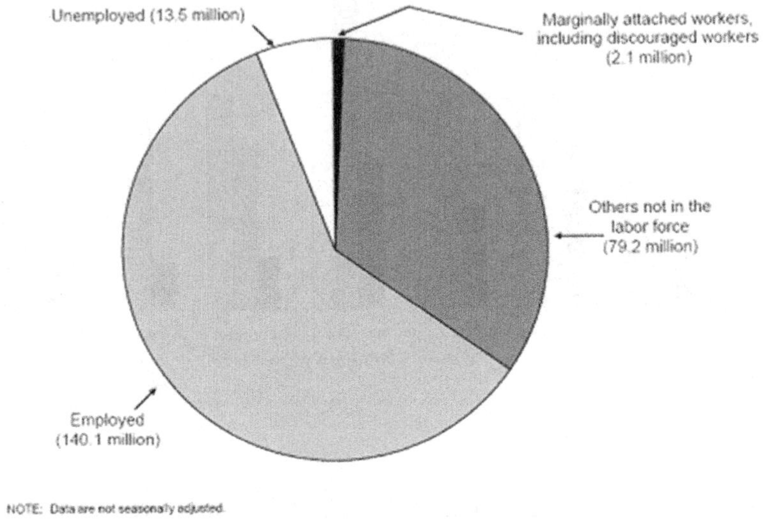


Source: U.S. Department of Labor, Bureau of Labor Statistics. 2009. Ranks of Discouraged Workers and Others Marginally Attached to the Labor Force Rise During Recession. See http://www.bls.gov/opub/ils/pdf/opbils74.pdf.

**15. Wealth Inequality**

The ownership of wealth among households in the U.S. became somewhat more concentrated since the 1980s. The top 10% of households controlled 68.2 percent of the total wealth in 1983 and 73.1% of the total wealth in 2007.Concentration of wealth in the U.S. between 1983 and 2007.

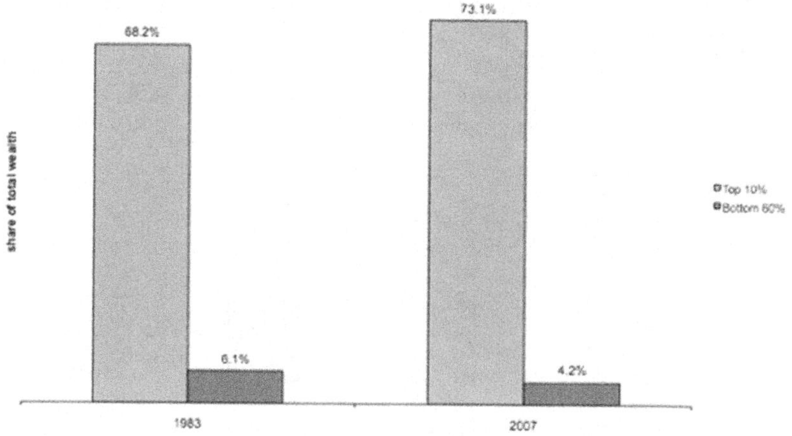


Source: Source: Edward N. Wolff, 2010. "Recent Trends in Household Wealth in the United States: Rising Debt and the Middle-Class Squeeze – An Update to 2007." Levy Economics Institute Working Paper No. 589. Annandale-on-Hudson, NY: Levy Economics Institute.

## 16. Intergenerational Income Mobility

Intergenerational income mobility can be measured by calculating the rate at which individuals move to income quintiles that are different than *[sic]* that of their families of origin. The proportion of sons who remained in the bottom quartile declined between 1961 and 1972 and stayed the same afterward.

**Family Background and Income in Adulthood (individuals age 30 to 59)**

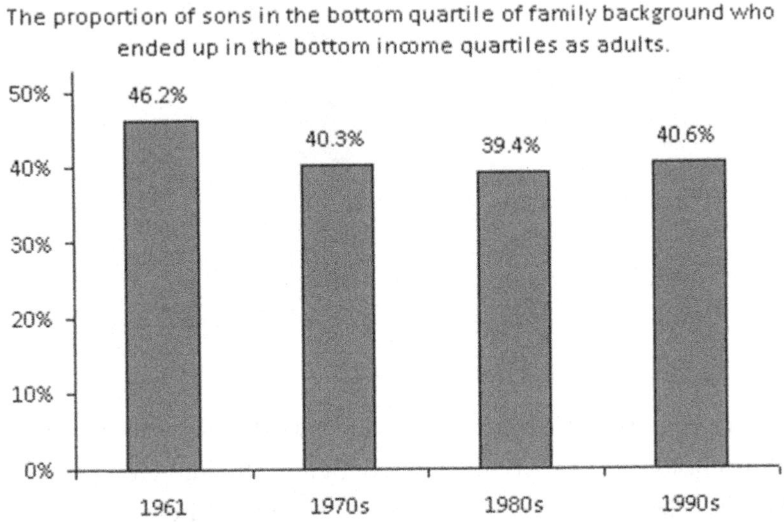


Source: Harding, David, Christopher Jencks, Leonard M. Lopoo, and Susan E. Mayer. 2008. "Family Background and Incomes in Adulthood." Pp. 505-515 in Social Stratification: Class, Race and Gender in Sociological Perspective, edited by David B. Grusky. Boulder, CO: Westview Press.

**17. Deregulation of the Labor Market**

The percentage of all wage and salary workers who are union members has declined from 24% in 1973 to 12.4% in 2008. The decline in the private sector was steeper than the decline in the public sector. At the same time as union membership declined, the real value of the minimum wage also fell by 25% in the 1980s, leading to a weakening influence of the minimum wage on the low-wage labor market. These two developments in combination may be understood as the foundation of the newly "deregulated."

**U.S. labor market. Private-sector union membership and real minimum wage, 1973-2008.**

Source: Barry T. Hirsch and David A. Macpherson. Union Membership and Coverage Database from the CPS. See http://www.unionstats.com; http://www.census.gov/compendia/statab/cats/labor_force_employment_earni...

**18. Job Losses**

Employment fell by 3.1 million jobs during 2008, and by another 4.7 million jobs in 2009. The job losses in the 2007-09 recession are more severe than in all prior recessions.

**Job losses in recent recessions, changes in total employment from beginning of recession.**

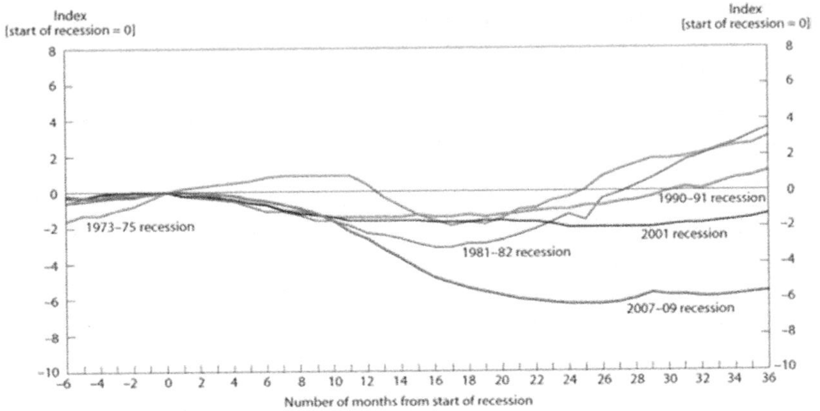


Source: Christopher J. Goodman and Steven M. Mance. 2011. Employment Loss and the 2007-09 Recession: An Overview. Monthly Labor Review. See: http://www.bls.gov/opub/mlr/2011/04/art1full.pdf

**19. Immigrants and Inequality**

Does immigration to the U.S. bring highly-skilled workers into the labor force or unskilled workers? The answer is both! The education distribution below indicates that immigrants are concentrated in both tails of the skill distribution.

**Characteristics of immigrant education enrollment in 2000.**

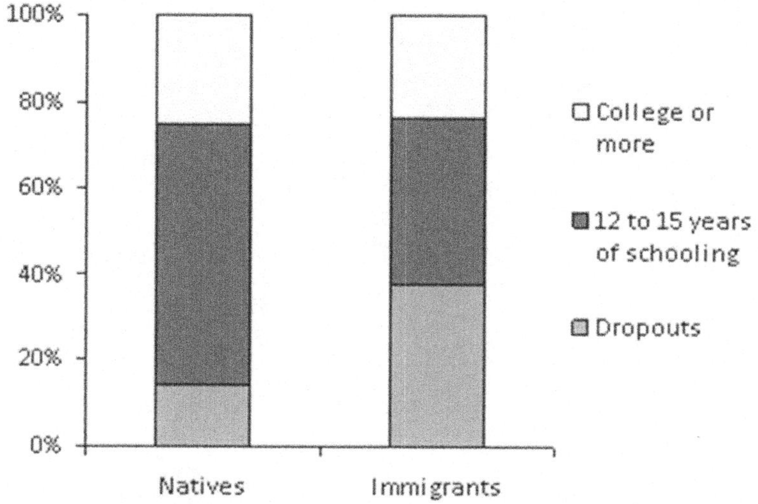


Source: David Card. 2009. Immigration and Inequality. Center for research and analysis of immigration. See http://eprints.ucl.ac.uk/14325/1/14325.pdf

**20. Incarceration**

The incarceration rate in the United States has grown so dramatically since the 1970s that the U.S. now has one of the highest rates in the world. The rise in incarceration has been especially prominent among young Black males and high school dropouts. As shown in this graph, a full 37% of those who are both young black males and high school dropouts are now in prison or jail, a rate that's more than three times higher than what prevailed in 1980.

**Percent of 20-34 year old men in prison or jail, by race, ethnicity, and educational attainment, 1980 and 2008.**

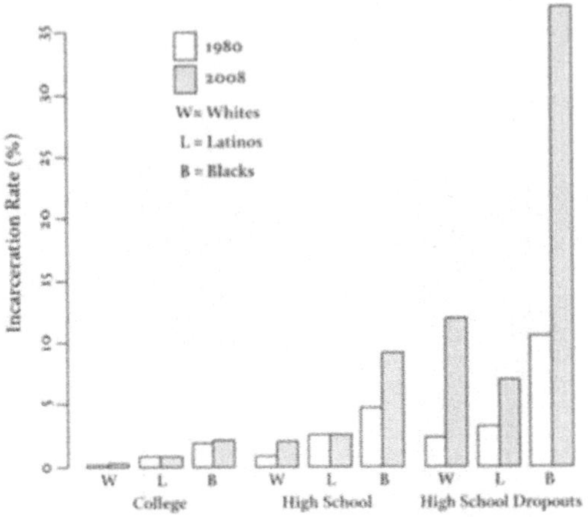


Source: Western, Bruce & Becky Pettit (2010). Incarceration and Social Inequality. Daedalus, 139(3), 8-19

One hundred years ago, you were considered middle class if you made $577 a year, according to TheCostofLiving.com. Today, many people make that much in a week. At least, according to the Bureau of Labor Statistics, the median weekly earnings of full-time workers for the first quarter of 2014 were $796.

But why does a disappearing middle class matter? "Why should I care about this thing called 'inequality'?" you might ask. The reason why you should care was clearly laid out by a Greek philosopher, Aristotle, 2,400 years ago. Aristotle pointed out that if the middle class disappeared, then the poor would become the majority. The poor tend to be less educated than the rich, and they tend to struggle just to make ends meet. If the poor are the majority, then in a democracy they will vote to take away the money from the rich!

So, what are the rich to do?

There is no universally recognized definition of middle class. There are federal poverty level guidelines, so if you happen to wonder if you're poor, you can consult the Department of Health & Human Services (not that you likely need guidelines to tell you if you're poor). But after that, you're on your own to decide if you're lower middle class, middle class, upper middle class, or in the fabulously wealthy territory. But to get us started thinking about financial status, a U.S. household with four people living off $23,850 or less is considered poor (Hawaii and Alaska, with higher costs of living, have different guidelines).

One helpful yardstick to judge whether you're middle class: Median household income was $51,017 in 2012, according to the most recent U.S. census data. Robert Reich, a professor of public policy at the University of California-Berkeley and former Secretary of Labor, has suggested the middle class be defined as households making 50 percent higher and lower than the median, which would mean the average middle class annual income is $25,500 to $76,500.

If you're in the middle of the middle, however—not lower or upper-middle class—that would be an income range between $39,764 and $64,582, says Aaron Pacitti, an assistant professor of economics at Siena College in Loudonville, N.Y.

The middle class is a political function created by tax brackets and the financial concept of owning a home that you are paying for and your name happens to be on the deed, but the bank has legal ownership rights to the property. Confusing? I would say so. Much of this was discussed by Noam Chomsky in the documentary Requiem for the American Dream where he discussed the "redesigning of the American economy" as pushback on the strides that were made during the civil rights movement.

The owners of society sought to increase the role of financial institutions. Moving the economy from a focus on manufacturing to money manipulation and the financialization of the economy. Trade systems were redesigned to put working people in competition with global workers, even the super-exploited worker, in places like China, India, etc. The highly paid professional does not have to endure this type of competition; their jobs are highly specialized and have innate barriers from certain forms of competition. This is not true for the middle class worker.

Free circulation of labor is the major component of a free market system. However, Alan Greenspan believed that worker insecurity or job insecurity keeps the workforce under control. Greenspan listed this as one element of his success as Federal Reserve Chairman, despite the fact this idea and practice is anti-American as it's a totalitarian idea.

Noam Chomsky also noted: the progress that was being made in America in the 50s and 60s, nearly all American life was improving at the same rate for the rich and the poor. However, after the 60s, the rights and opportunity that were given to the poor and middle class infuriated the elite; they wanted their plutocracy back. Therefore, the elite begin their campaign to "shift the burden" to the Precarious Proletariat. The working people of the world live increasingly precarious lives; the rich do not pay many taxes and through controlling the electorate and legislative process, they pay less and less, shifting the burden for maintaining the country to the middle and lower classes. Most of the taxes are paid on consumption and not on dividends of investments or estates.

The last point that I will mention by Noam Chomsky is the elite "attack on solidarity." Adam Smith, the author of Wealth of Nations, believed that sympathy is a fundamental human trait (which is also true for every religious and ethical leader of every generation). The masters of the universe want you to only care about yourself and no one else; their goal is to have everyone to think this way. They attack Social Security, Medicare, and public schools, by eliminating funding.

Their strategies are working, but the solutions lie within a few areas. The primary area is ensuring that the poor and middle class become economically astute, understanding their economic power and the true power of compound interest. These lower and middle classes need access to advice, at the same level as their wealthy counterparts.

When considering the engagement of a wealth management firm, how do you determine if the value of an advisor justifies the cost—or if you are better off just handling your own finances? Until recently, the answer to this question was not always clear. However, in 2013, Morningstar, an independent investment research organization, published a groundbreaking analysis in a white paper entitled *Alpha, Beta, and Now…Gamma.* Advisers can add additional income to investor portfolios by helping their clients make better financial decisions in five key areas. The Morningstar study quantified this value at a 29% increase in retirement income, or the equivalent of generating 1.82% of additional return annually. What may be surprising to some is that the selection of investments is only a portion of the overall value derived from advisors. The five key areas discussed in the Morningstar study are asset allocation, withdrawal strategy, tax efficiency, product selection, and liability investing (or investing toward a specific goal).James Hopkins, a Forbes contributor, noted: "Only 52% of pre-retirees and 44% of retirees consult a financial planner or adviser according to a new report, Understanding and Managing the Risks of Retirement, from the Society of Actuaries (SOA), which discusses the findings of their Retirement Risk Survey conducted in 2013. The report highlights a variety of concerns faced by both pre-and post-retirees, including concerns about health care, long-term care, inflation, and running out of money in retirement. With roughly 96% of pre-retirees and 89% of retirees responding that they are concerned to some degree about their long-term financial future in retirement, it is troubling that only about 50% of people meet with a financial adviser. Confidence and peace of mind are just two of the more obvious reasons to seek the services of a financial adviser. Most people in the baby-boomer generation are not confident that they will have enough money for retirement. According to an IRI 2014 survey, baby-boomers with financial advisers are twice as likely to feel confident about their retirement savings as those without an adviser.

> Adding confidence to one's retirement plan is not the only thing that financial advisers do. In fact, financial advisers are well equipped to help America reduce its retirement income shortfall of nearly $4.3 trillion. For example, an international HSBC study, The Future of Retirement, in 2011 showed that those with financial plans accumulated nearly 250% more retirement savings than those without a financial plan in place. Furthermore, nearly 44% of those who have a financial plan in place save more money each year for retirement.

Even if you have a financial plan in place and a retirement income plan, financial advisers can still add value. For instance, Carol Bogosian, ASA, Member of the SOA's Committee on Post-Retirement Needs and Risks, said "people who do plan for retirement may have a short-term planning horizon and a focus on day-to-day living expenses. The ability to pay monthly bills often is their main financial planning input for the decision to retire." Furthermore, Bogosian went on to note "financial planners can help address difficult long-term planning items and provide guidance for a better planning position."

Financial advisers offer a tremendous amount of value by dealing with extremely complex tax issues, investment choices, and emotional decisions impacting one's financial well-being. Furthermore, they make people more secure for retirement, increase their client's wealth, and help people feel more confident about their financial status. However, not all financial planners are created equal and a few tips should be followed when looking for a financial planner.

"...Financial planners are not just for the wealthy, but they do cost money. In fact, because of evolutions in the compensation models used by financial planners, there are financial planners available for almost everyone. There are planners out there that focus exclusively on high wealth, middle wealth, and low wealth individuals..." The system is not designed to assist or to help the middle and lower classes economically. Therefore, good, quality advice is needed to navigate this ever-changing, confusing, economic jungle. However, advice alone is not the sole culprit, but it is a key element to fighting inequality.

Laura Shin, a writer for Forbes, noted that the wealth gap between white and black Americans is quite significant. The typical white household has 16 times the wealth of a black one. The typical black household now has just 6% of the wealth of the typical white household; the typical Latino household has just 8%, according to a recent study called, "The Racial Wealth Gap: Why Policy Matters," by Demos, a public policy organization promoting democracy and equality, and the Institute on Assets and Social Policy.

In absolute terms, the median white household had $111,146 in wealth holdings in 2011, compared to $7,113 for the median black household and $8,348 for the median Latino household (all figures come from the U.S. Census Bureau Survey of Income and Program Participation). She goes on to focus on three areas as the cause of this disparity:

**Homeownership**

"For most U.S. families, a home usually comprises the largest portion of their assets. Homeownership is the central vehicle Americans use to store wealth, so homeownership and access to homeownership are at the heart of that widening wealth gap," says [Catherine] Ruetschlin. But disparities in homeownership fall along racial and ethnic lines. Seventy-three percent of whites own a home, compared to 47% of Latinos and 45% of blacks. The median white homeowner's house is worth $85,800 compared to $50,000 for black homeowners and $48,000 for Latino homeowners.

**Figure 2. Homeownership Rates**

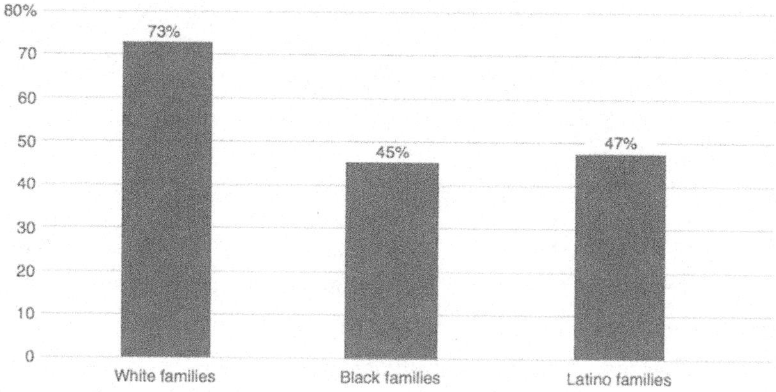


Source: Survey of Income and Program Participation (SIPP), 2008 Panel Wave 10, 2011

Much of that disparity comes from the gap in the home values in white neighborhoods versus the neighborhoods where people of color live. The roots of the gulf stem at least as far back as the 1934 National Housing Act, which redlined black neighborhoods, marking them as credit risks. Though redlining was outlawed in the '60s, the effect persists today in the form of neighborhoods consisting mostly of people of color that have high poverty rates, low home values and declining infrastructure. Discriminatory lending also exists today: Mortgages obtained by households of color tend to have higher interest rates. Even as recently as 2012, Wells Fargo admitted it had steered black and Latino households into subprime mortgages but had offered white borrowers with similar credit profiles prime mortgages.

## Education

A college education is all but required to flourish in the labor market, establish financial stability, and build wealth. But the gap in college attainment by whites versus blacks and Latinos has widened over the last decade. In 2011, 34% of whites completed a four-year college degree, whereas just 20% of blacks and 13% of Hispanics did.

One obstacle is the surge in college costs over recent years, forcing households to take on significant debt to send students [*sic*] to college.

But obtaining a bachelor's degree isn't enough for a black or Hispanic person to escape the racial wealth gap. The return on investment in college is much higher for whites than for blacks and Hispanics: A white family at the median sees a return of $55,869 from completing a four-year degree. A black family sees $4,846 and Hispanic family $4,191.

**Figure 11. Median Wealth Return to College Graduation**

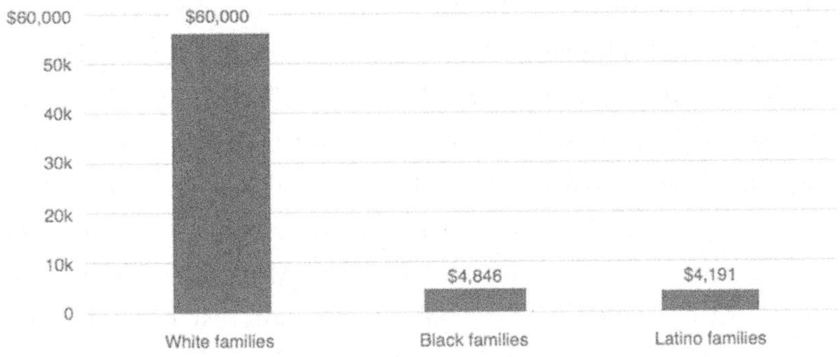


Source: Survey of Income and Program Participation (SIPP), 2008 Panel Wave 10, 2011

## Labor Markets

Labor markets can provide economic security through earned income, employer-provided health coverage, paid leave and workplace retirement plans. But inequality in the labor market is responsible for 20% of the growth in the racial wealth gap in the last 25 years, and unemployment another 9%. Disparate outcomes in the labor market can come from employment discrimination, geographic barriers to jobs and differing levels of social capital.

The typical white family earns $50,400, while the typical black family earns $32,038, and the typical Latino family, $36,840.

"In the labor market, the wealth return to a dollar of income is first determined by how much of that income you have the opportunity to save," says Ruetschlin. "If you are facing a wealth gap of 80 cents for every dollar a white family makes, that makes you 20% less able to put that dollar into savings, because you may need all of those dollars to fill your consumption needs."

Additionally, black and Latino families earn a lower return on their incomes, meaning they are less able to turn each additional dollar of income into wealth. A white family will typically see a return of $19.51 for each dollar earned, while a black family will see only $4.80 in return and Latino families $3.63.

**Figure 17. Median Wealth Return to an Additional $1 of Income**

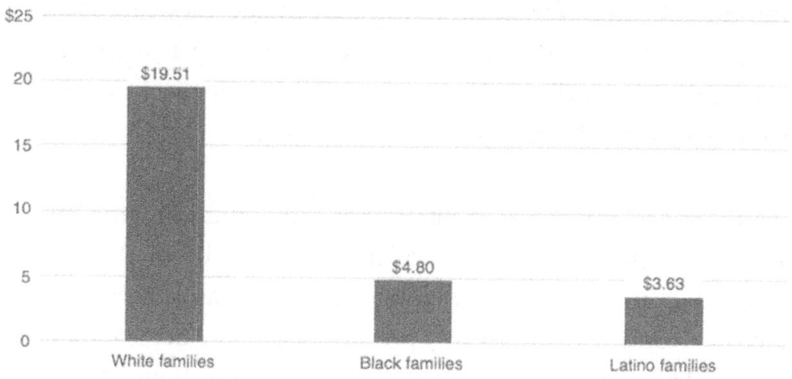


Source: Survey of Income and Program Participation (SIPP), 2008 Panel Wave 10, 2011

Causes include the fact that blacks and Latinos are less likely to have jobs that include employer-sponsored health care, a retirement plan or paid time off. The net result is that families of color spend more of their savings on dealing with life's emergencies such as out-of-pocket health care. Or, they have fewer wealth-building vehicles, such as tax-advantaged accounts, available to them.

The origin of wealth inequality can be easily found. Generally it comes down to these four questions. 1. How much do you start with? 2. How much income do you make? 3. How much of your income do you save? 4. What is your rate of return on your savings? Again, the key is how much money you keep and the assets/ investments you own. According to the data, people with higher incomes tend to save more, meaning they build wealth more rapidly. Second, people with higher incomes tend to have less risk aversion, meaning they are more willing to invest in assets like stocks (which get higher average rates of return, although they are risky) rather than safe assets like savings accounts and CDs that get low rates of return. In other words, giving the poor and middle class more income will boost the amount they are *able* to save, the percentage they are *willing* to save, and the *return* they get on those savings. Part of the reason America's wealth distribution is so unequal in the first place is that our income distribution is very unequal.

But there are reasons to believe that redistribution can't fix the entire problem, or even most of it. If you do the math, you discover that in the long run, income levels and initial wealth (factors 1 and 2 from above) are not the main determinants of wealth. They are dwarfed by factors 3 and 4—savings rates and rates of return. The most potent way to get more wealth to the poor and middle class is to get these people to save more of their income, and to invest in assets with higher average rates of return.

As I mentioned, income redistribution helps these things a bit, but it doesn't account for the whole difference. The rich probably save more than the poor for many more reasons besides the simple fact that they're rich. In fact, being willing to save more is probably a big part of how the rich got rich in the first place. "Cheap" is an insult, but being cheap is how you get rich. If you consume everything you earn, your consumption will be higher today, but lower twenty years down the road; in our consumption-focused society, a lot of people are caught in this trap. We must save more! Even though we live in the era of over-consumption, we must be willing to count every cent and become more economically savvy. Yes, we are back to receiving financial advice, but we're adding more elements, which are extremely important. Another key is of course saving. However, this is important, but it must be tied to education. This means that more financial education in public schools is a must.

I'm not talking about teaching kids the Capital Asset Pricing Model. I mean what Bob Shiller calls "basic Suze Orman stuff"—how to make a monthly budget, what "saving" and "borrowing" mean, how wealth builds over time, how to avoid borrowing lots of money at high interest rates (e.g. credit cards and payday loans), etc. The new Consumer Financial Protection Bureau can help a lot with this, too, by preventing companies from tricking poor people into taking out high-interest debt. In addition to "nudging" middle-class and poor Americans to save more, we can help them get a better return on their assets—the second thing that has a huge effect on wealth in the long run. This means helping middle-class people invest in stocks without paying high fees. The first part of this is teaching middle-class people to avoid making frequent changes in their stock portfolios. Studies show that individual investors consistently lose money when they try to buy and sell and buy and sell, mostly because they tend to ignore trading costs. So financial education should teach people to seek advice and training for things they don't understand, including understanding that accruing wealth is not a trip; it's a journey.

The last key element is discipline. We must be willing to learn and practice wealth accumulation habits, as well as recognize habits that are not conducive to wealth building. Kalen Bruce identified 10 differences between middle-class and the wealthy:

**1. The middle class, live comfortably, the rich embrace being uncomfortable**

> "Be willing to be uncomfortable. Be comfortable being uncomfortable. It may get tough, but it's a small price to pay for living a dream."
>
> —Peter McWilliams

It's comfortable to work a "safe" job. It's comfortable to work for someone else. The middle class think being comfortable means being happy, but the rich realize that extraordinary things happen when we put ourselves in uncomfortable situations. Starting your own business is a risk and risks can be uncomfortable, but a little risk is what it takes to create wealth and achieve superior results.

Step out of your comfort zone. Look at all your options. You will have to be at least a little uncomfortable if you want to become rich. You might even have to fail and that's great, because if you're not failing, you're not doing much.

**2. The middle class live above their means, the rich live below**

> "There is no dignity quite so impressive, and no one independence quite so important, as living within your means."
>
> —Calvin Coolidge

You won't catch the average millionaire in a $100,000 car or a multi-million dollar home. The rich don't spend their money on depreciating liabilities; they spend their money on appreciating assets and they live below their means. On average, the rich drive cars that are a few years old and they don't buy them new, according to studies done in the book, "The Millionaire Next Door" Even if they can "afford" that fancy new Escalade, they usually don't buy it.

Remember, if you earn $1,000,000/year and you spend $1,000,000/year, you're still broke.

**3. The middle class climb the corporate ladder, the rich own the ladder**

> "The richest people in the world look for and build networks; everyone else looks for work."
>
> —Robert Kiyoski

**4. The middle class are friends with everyone, the rich choose wisely**

> "It's better to hang out with people better than you. Pick out associates whose behavior is better than yours and you'll drift in that direction."
>
> —Warren Buffet

The rich understand that when you surround yourself with successful people, your own success will follow. Likewise, surrounding yourself with unsuccessful people tends to have the anticipated effect. Your income is usually the average of the incomes of your three closest friends. If you want to earn more, hang around people who earn more. It's all about aligning your mindset with the mindset of successful people. If you want to be rich, you have to think rich.

**5. The middle class work to earn; the rich work to learn**

> "When you are young, work to learn, not to earn."
>
> —Robert Kiyosaki

The middle class are easily persuaded to change jobs when someone offers more money. The rich understand that working isn't about the money, especially in the early years. It's about developing the skills and traits you need to develop to become rich. That may mean working a sales job to better understand the world of selling. Or it could mean you work at a bank to better understand accounting. If you want to be rich, you should be working to learn the skills you need to become rich. Most rich people didn't get there by earning a high salary.

**6. The middle class have things; the rich have money**

> "Too many people spend money they haven't earned, to buy things they don't want, to impress people that they don't like."
>
> —Will Rogers

Stop buying things and start focusing on keeping, saving, and investing the money you earn. If you are a shopaholic, start shopping for assets. Become interested in investing then look for bargains on stocks and businesses instead of shoes and electronics. That being said, it's not all about saving your money.

**7. The middle class are emotional with money, the rich are logical**

> "Only when you combine sound intellect with emotional discipline do you get rational behavior."
>
> —Warren Buffet

Steve Siebold interviewed over 1,200 of the world's wealthiest people over the past 30 years for his book How Rich People Think, and according to him there are more than 100 differences in how rich people look at money compared to the middle class. One of the key differences he found was that the middle class see money through the eyes of emotion, but the rich see money through the eyes of logic. Making emotional financial decisions will ruin your finances. Warren Buffett explains that investing has much more to do with controlling your emotions, than it has to do with money. Emotions are what cause people to buy high and sell low. Emotions create dangerous business deals. Leave emotions out of this and turn to logic.

**8. The middle class underestimate their potential, the rich set huge goals**

> "Set your goals high, and don't stop till you get there."
> —Bo Jackson

The middle class set goals. Sometimes. It's the capacity of the goals that differ from the middle class to the rich. The middle class set safe goals that are easily obtainable. The rich set goals that seem impossible, difficult or crazy. But they know they are achievable. It all comes back to having the proper mindset.

When you're setting your goals, ask yourself if they could be bigger. Ask yourself if that's really all you can do or if you can do more. I think you can do more.

**9. The middle class believe in hard work, the rich believe in leverage**

> "It is much easier to put existing resources to better use than to develop resources where they do not exist."
> —George Soros

Hard work is a necessity, for all of us. If you want to reach the top (whatever that may be for you), you've got to put in the work. The problem is that hard work alone will rarely make you rich. You can't become rich by doing it all yourself. You have to use leverage to truly become rich and stay that way. Leverage works in many ways, from outsourcing to investing. The more leverage you can incorporate, the more time you will free up to work on the things that really matter in your business and your life.

**10. Some differences between the middle class and the rich are vast, while others may seem simple and minor.** The fact is that if you want to become rich, you have to think like the rich and do the things the rich do.

# IS THE SYSTEM FLAWED, OR ARE WE?

> "We can't impose our will on a system. We can listen to what the system tells us, and discover how its properties and our values can work together to bring forth something much better than could ever be produced by our will alone."
>
> —Donella H. Meadows, Thinking in Systems:

After 14 years on Florida's death row, Frank Lee Smith died of cancer in January 2000, before he was exonerated of rape and murder. The DNA results not only cleared Smith of the crime, but also identified the true perpetrator, Eddie Lee Mosley.
According to the Innocence Project, 311 people in U.S. history, 18 of whom were sentenced to the death penalty, have been freed after DNA evidence proved them innocent.

The average DNA exonoree has served 13.6 years behind bars.

In 2013, nine men were exonerated. Flawed eyewitness testimony is a factor in 76% of wrongful convictions. False confessions play a role in a quarter of them.

> "DNA testing is not always an option. First, biological evidence—hair, blood, semen, or saliva—must be present and preserved. In 90-95% of major felonies, it's not. If it is, either the prosecutor must consent to have the testing done, or the court must order it. In 19% of cases, this doesn't happen. Lastly, the testing must yield

a conclusive result, an outcome reached in fewer than 20% of cases."

—Laura Dimon

The Federal Trade Commission has rightly intensified scrutiny of the companies that provide the criminal background checks used by most firms and corporations to screen job applicants. In too many cases, the reports are out of date and incomplete, causing job seekers who may have been arrested but never charged—or who have had their cases expunged or even dismissed—to be unfairly locked out of the job market.

The new oversight is important, given that these companies sometimes ignore a federal law that requires them to make sure that the reports are accurate. But more oversight is not enough. Congress must also focus on the flawed practices of the Federal Bureau of Investigation, the nation's most important provider of criminal background data. Its data, too, has unfairly damaged the prospects of people seeking work.
[…]
F.B.I. background checks are widely viewed as the gold standard but are in fact woefully flawed, often based on fallible and incomplete data submitted to the bureau by state and local law enforcement. Those agencies do a good job of transmitting arrest and fingerprint data but a terrible job of including information on the cases' outcome. For example, the United States attorney general in 2006 found that about half the records in the F.B.I. database were missing final disposition information.

> Employers who used those records would not have seen that an applicant with an arrest record was never convicted.
>
> The law project report includes examples of workers who were either turned away from jobs or fired based on faulty F.B.I. background information. Federal data show that more than 90 percent of workers who appealed denials of security clearances from the Transportation Security Administration were successful, because the F.B.I. records had been inaccurate or incomplete.—New York Times, Editorial Board. I live on the west bank of the Indian River Lagoon on Florida's East Coast. Across the Lagoon, in the distance, is Kennedy Space Center. For years, I walked out on my dock and watched space shuttle launches.
>
> The disaster resulted from failure of an O-ring, a rubberlike seal in the right solid fuel booster rocket. Brittle from the cold, it allowed hot gas to leak and eat away hardware until it burned through the external fuel tank and ignited its contents, a small design problem with a big consequence.

American education has a problem, and, left unaddressed, its consequences will be catastrophic. The problem is an appalling, embarrassing, inexcusable rate of childhood poverty, one of the worst in the developed world. Compare our 22.4 % rate with Sweden at 2.6%. Poverty being the single best predictor of test scores, that's pretty far from a level playing field for America's educators. The poverty situation is so dire it almost seems inappropriate to call attention to a second, very different problem.

I do so, first, because I believe the problem is far too serious to continue to ignore; second, because I want to toss a wrench into the corporate gears now grinding out destructive, market-based school reform policies. I'd like to think that the amateurs promoting today's simplistic reform policies are smart enough to realize they're in over their heads, that American education has problems they've never even thought about.

> "Call this one a design problem. It may seem small, but its consequences are huge. Solve the poverty problem, and America's scores on international tests will once more be at or near the top. But leave the design problem in place, and the scores of none of the top performers will mean what they could and should mean.
>
> The design problem? Traditional instruction is dumping poorly organized information on the young, and they can't process it. The problem isn't the amount of information—the brain isn't a bucket that can overflow. The problem is the information's incoherence..."
>
> —Marion Brady, veteran teacher, administrator, curriculum designer, author, Washington Post

Today, we are inundated with many messages about our current American systems. Whether we are discussing our judicial, political, educational, or economic policies, there is usually a debate that ensues, where each side attempts to label the other. Characterizations are rarely helpful because it strips away your individuality and establishes you as just another member of some extreme faction. No one is 100% anything but human. We are diverse and are made up of vastly different experiences, and to start by categorizing a person nullifies our ability to perceive the complexities of one's spectrum of experiences. We must revisit the art of listening first before we assume. We must go back to hearing from and studying an assortment of individuals before assuming any level of collective understanding. Be that as it may, first I want to take a look at systems and investigate their viability in modern society. Second, I hope to present a new perspective on business as a whole, for our current one has left us badly bruised.

For example, we are living in the time of "Big Data" where tech enterprises collect bits and pieces of a plethora of your daily choices and claim to know you and your intimate desires (this is obscenely arrogant and out of step with the truth). From this data, these companies place you within clusters which they sell to other corporate enterprises. I removed myself from Facebook once I realized that over 2/3 of the people who had friended me, I didn't know or remember meeting. I guess that is what happens when you entrust your social interaction to some whiz kid who struggles with organic interactions. Facebook is a social platform (system) that simply amplifies the worst and best in each user. If you are a gifted liar, and generally you lie to 25 people a week, being on Facebook will not change that; it will give you the opportunity to lie to millions. The reciprocal is true for truth-tellers. However, a Facebook friend is not the same as a real friend; at best, it is only a shadow of what friendship is. The danger is that in watering down the meaning of a friend and replacing the old meaning with the feckless new, Facebook attempts to mimic organic interactions and relationship building. It is not the same.

A system is "an organized, purposeful structure that consists of interrelated and interdependent elements (components, entities, factors, members, parts, etc.). These items continually influence one another (directly or indirectly) to maintain their activity and the existence of the system, to achieve the goal of the system."

> "Human systems are human modes of action which are dependent for their continuance on a fundamental tacit agreement among men to continue to act in the same way; and such agreement implies that those who continue to enact any particular system must be prepared to meet and to accept its disadvantages as well as its advantages; for in the struggle for advantage there must always be the corresponding disadvantage; in the battle of human interest there must always be both victory and defeat."
>
> —James Allen

Since nearly the beginning of time, men have used systems to do everything, to structure, influence, protect, and communicate and to achieve the desired goal. Currently, in the world, there is a widespread consensus in opposition to systems. These systems are seen as the cause for the controlling and limiting aspects that rule over humanity. Many believe that the political, social, and the economic policies have orchestrated such evils as widespread poverty, limiting of opportunity, and inequalities; portraying the system as some wicked ruler, enslaving and crushing innocent and unwilling humanity; as if the system is some abstract creation, coming from aliens for different beings of some kind. Policies created by humankind are not separate from human desires and needs; they are the visible manifestation of those wants and needs. A system is nothing more than a reflection of the mode of action of its creators and community. It's a contract between participating parties outlining the terms and how the enforcing of those conditions will take place.

James Allen once said, "As men act, so systems appear; as they cease to act, so they disappear." Human beings, who are engaged in a system wittingly or unwittingly, have accepted that system and must accept the output of that system positively or negatively. If someone disagrees with a system, they must not participate, or they must find a way to change the system or create a new one that better serves their purpose. For this to happen, they must find others who are willing to participate in this new augmented system. The larger moral issue is that we often attempt to separate ourselves from the systems that we create and actively participate in and when the output is negative we blame the systems and not ourselves. Many when confronted with the negative outcome of a system they participated in, often state. "Don't blame me; blame the system."

Take 20 individuals who have chosen to participate in a game; they outlined and have agreed to abide by the rules set forth. It is understood by all that those who were better prepared, smarter, more industrious, and favored by chance are most likely to win the majority of the spoils. Therefore, they all understand that those who remain will fight over the leftovers. They further know that the individuals who had success could and likely would continue to build more fortunes at a faster rate than anyone else until someone better suited with a better method chose to participate, or the rules of the game were changed to put them at a disadvantage.

Would it be fair for either the winner or the loser to hold them blameless in the outcome? Now, it cannot be said of the winners that they are guilty of exploiting the losers; nor can it be said of the losers that they are the innocent victims of the system or game, in which they were willing participants. In the actions of these 20 men there is neither innocence nor guilt, but an agreement in a method, with its foreseeable results: namely, the reaping of its advantages on the one hand, and the suffering from its disadvantages on the other.

From my perspective, systems are not inherently evil, but in practice can become evil based on the participants. Systems are made up of individuals and can rise or fall to the level of the character and moral code of its participants. However, each participant has a responsibility, once involved in a system, to operate at the highest level of character and moral code. For the participants not to do so will pervert the output of the system. What we must not engage in is blaming the system when we don't like the outcome, when one's self is involved in the very same order. The participants are to blame and through participating, have agreed to abide by the rules and accept the outcome. No system will benefit all, but the result of all operations good or bad are foreseeable. If you don't like the system, don't engage. Sound harsh? Hardly.

> "That human being seeks their well-being, and that of those close to them is not an especially interesting discovery. What is important is that this universal aspect of human nature persists no matter what economic system is in place; it merely expresses itself in different forms."
>
> —Thomas Wood.

In the writings of Ayn Rand in Atlas Shrugged (published in 1957), Rand set out to explain her philosophy. Rand's philosophy was known as Objectivism, which was and remains very controversial. Objectivism criticized a lot of beliefs and views from Christianity to communism and was in line with the fact that Rand was a devout atheist.

Atlas Shrugged starts off with the world in a conundrum; the government is becoming insanely oppressive, and the economy is tanking. To the rescue appear two businesspeople who just might hold the answers to the country's problems: Dagny Taggart and Hank Reardon. The two decide to build a railroad to provide Colorado the train service it requires. Dagny and Hank are successful in their plan. However, they need assistance from other businesspeople, most of all the John Galt line, which uses an alloy metal that Hank invented. The economic depression is worsening in the U.S., and the world is wondering about the unexplained disappearance of talented men. The question begins to surface—who is John Galt? Many believe perhaps he has something to do with the missing gifted individuals. Dagny and Hank push forward with their current problems at hand. Of course, as in most stories with a male and female antagonist, the two begin a romantic relationship and a quest to find the inventor of a high-tech motor that could change the world. The economy continues its descent downwards, and the government with its shady politicians and businesspeople pass a series of laws that reduce and restrict people's freedoms. Of course, these rules are aimed at the most creative and successful of business leaders.

Dagny and Hank are still together, yet begin to deal with a personal quest. Dagny begins her search for the destroyer of the world, and Hank starts to re-evaluate his life and moral code.

Dagny follows a vital scientist who she thinks may disappear as the others have. Her plane crashes, and she finds herself in a secret hideaway that is owned by John Galt and his fellow strikers. Dagny calls the valley Atlantis; she considers that Galt is the creator of the "destroyer" and the motor.

Galt has called all of the talented people together, to teach the government a lesson. He wants them to see the results of their oppressive policies and refers to them as the "looters."

Of course, Galt has always loved Dagny, and she falls for Galt. Shortly after that, she goes to end her relationship with Hank. Later, Hank disappears to Atlantis also. After things in the world become even worse, Galt makes a long radio address; the thinkers won't return, Galt says, until human society recognizes an individual's right to live his own life. Only when the moral code of self-sacrifice is rejected will the thinkers be free to create, and only then will they return.

But Galt is captured by the government shortly after that and is tortured. The rulers attempt to convince Galt to take charge of the country's economy. He refuses. Dagny, helped by Hank, Francisco, and other strikers, rescues Galt, and the group flees for Atlantis as the country's infrastructure collapses. Dagny and Galt are united. Shortly after, the final collapse of the looters' regime occurs, and the men of the mind or the strikers prepare to return.

It is assumed that they would start a society and design systems that were more in line with their beliefs, leaving the less productive and unproductive to fend for themselves. I found the story to be very interesting and often wondered what would eventually happen to the people who were left behind. After some thought, it was quite clear that the more productive of the remaining classes would rise to assume control. So, it is nearly a foregone conclusion; if this new group became frustrated with the society and regulation around the economic system, they could leave, thereby repeating a cycle, until the most unproductive would eventually be left to themselves, in a society where all the ills of the barren would escort them to extinction. However, there would be one constant: the most productive and industrious would consistently rise to assume control. No matter what system or society, the unproductive would find themselves at the bottom, and this would be a just outcome.

Isn't this the current state of affairs in America today? Productive individuals often leave their neighborhoods, communities, cities, and states based off of how many unproductive people or businesses are located there. Therefore, we see the best communities seemingly getting better, by having highly productive people in one city. Over time, this will consistently foster higher productivity. Having communities with unproductive people promotes a decline. It is Atlas Shrugged in America today. People move away from high-crime areas, inadequate school systems, poor business districts and these areas are notoriously unproductive areas.

The seed of our nation is its people. The ideas and principles make up the ground that these seeds are sown in. Each child, as he grows up, seeks out his place within his family, neighborhood, community, etc. As he grows, his level of productivity will start to separate him from others. This separation in most cases will allow him to be around more productive people, which in turn increases his productivity. As his future appears to take a definite shape, so will his access to more people willing to assist him on his road to success. The opposite is true for the unproductive; fewer people are ready to attach themselves to a train that is seemingly headed for mediocrity or worse.

What we must understand is that we must think of our neighborhoods in the context of gardening or farming. Farmers use a concept called crop rotation. "There is the practice of growing a series of unique or different types of crops in the same area in sequenced seasons. It is done so that the soil of farms is not acclimated to only one set of nutrients. Growing the same crop in the same place for many years in a row depletes the soil of certain nutrients. With rotation, a crop that leaches the soil of one kind of nutrient is followed during the next growing season by a dissimilar crop that returns that nutrient to the soil or draws a different ratio of nutrients. Also, crop rotation mitigates the buildup of pathogens and pests that often occurs when one species is continuously cropped, and can also improve soil structure and fertility by increasing biomass from various root structures."

What I am proposing is not gentrification or re-gentrification, which is a replacement of less affluent with more affluent. In practice, we see this often happen in urban areas where the communities are allowed to fail, only to have those same communities sold for a significantly reduced price, then renovated and sold to a more affluent clientele. What I am speaking of is active management, which is done consistently and often—evaluating the viability of the community and ensuring the city take the necessary steps to stay solvent. We must manage systems to maximize their returns, because if we don't, then we will have more of what we have today in our country.

Nature at once ends the life of that which has become useless. Her economy is never in error, and she will not hold on to things that are no longer of service; this is only valid if nature itself is killing things off and not humanity through its misuse of the environment. What does all of this mean? I believe this affirms my earlier thought. Systems are not innately evil; they rise or fall to the moral level of the participants in that order. However, nature gives it to us in the purest form. The unproductive must not be upheld by the productive; the barren, the useless, must meet their ultimate fate—death. However, within a community or family, nature teaches us something completely different. They guard and protect their own until it proves to be a detriment to their society or their family. They understand that these systems need to be actively managed to produce the desired results. We must not kill off or get rid of a group of people due to our mismanagement of systems, resources, and environments.

I am not saying that systems do not have inherent flaws built in. I am assuming quite the opposite: that systems are created by flawed individuals for flawed purposes which means the system itself will be flawed. However flawed the system may be, the future of the system lies in the hand of those who have created it and are participating in that order. All operations must be actively managed, and at some point will need adjustments, and others may need to be renovated or completely torn down and reconstructed. The trick is staying aligned with your original goals and adjusting when those goals change.

However, the blame game must cease, we must all take responsibility for the systems we inhabit. James Allen noted:

"Now, it cannot be said of the winners that they are guilty of exploiting and crushing down the losers; nor can it be said of the losers that they are the innocent victims of the system of gambling in which they are engaged. In the mental attitude and actions of men, there is neither innocence nor guilt, but a mutual engagement in a method, with its inevitable results, namely, the reaping of its advantages, on the one hand, the suffering from its disadvantages on the other.

In like manner, of the various systems in which men have involved themselves, there are no innocent victims, no guilty tyrants. Victims there are if men choose to apply that term to the defeated, or to those who, for the time being, are suffering loss; but they are the victims of their deeds, and not of an overruling and compelling injustice outside themselves. Those outside the system- that is, those who do not encourage and propagate it by their acts- remain untouched, and uninjured by it. So if our present commercial system should be a "system of greed," as many social reformers style it, then not by any possibility whatever could any but the greedy be injured by it. Doubtless, there is much greed in the world, for in its present stage of evolution humanity is learning its lessons largely along narrow paths; but greed can never have any existence in external "systems," it can only exist in human hearts; nor can greed injure any but the greedy. Commercialism is free from greed in the hands of those who have destroyed greed in themselves, but they who are greedy will taint everything even religion with their impure condition."

If I deem a system as unrighteous, I must first withdraw my consent from that system. I must not participate. My choices are to withdraw from the system or oppose that system. No other choices are acceptable; any choice other than those two will only give my consent. Thomas Jefferson noted, "If a law is unjust, a man is not only right to disobey. He is obligated to do so." Martin Luther King Jr. wrote, one who breaks an unjust law that conscience tells him is unjust … is, in reality, expressing the highest respect for the law. I believe that King's and Jefferson's statements are true for systems also. As a society, we must oppose unjust policies, and as individuals, we must resist injustices no matter where we find them. Whether it is in life, business or within systems that may benefit us or within ourselves, we must confront all injustice that contradicts God's law.

So, now we have taken most of the blame from systems themselves and begun to at least consider that we as individuals hold a larger proportion of the blame. As I mentioned earlier, nature has provided us examples of elegant and intelligent designs and models that have lasted for centuries, that evolved and never became outdated. Perhaps, when building or creating systems, we have been more concerned about how that system will ultimately benefit ourselves rather than the overall design and functionality for all participants. The focus has to be on the paradigm through which we view the system, design, and functionality. In others words what are the limits of a system, and can we be sure that the creator and the user of that system live by a high moral code, have kept our individuality and privacy at the forefront, while creating systems that are functional, but not addictive nor have the capacity to manipulate the user. I know this is a difficult task, but one, we must consider.

How much time do we spend on these new social platforms, when these systems have become addicting for many? Surprisingly, life is short, and we have no time to waste on trivial things like fear or worry: much less time to spend on others' personal matters. American adults consume more than 11 hours per day watching, reading, listening to or merely interacting with media, according to a new study by market research group Nielsen. That's up from nine hours, 32 minutes just four years ago. How many people were born to spend their life watching television, or surfing the internet? Please raise your hand, if you believe that you were born to spend nearly half a day on media? Not likely, so how do we allow so many things of little value to consume so much of our attention and time? Now, this would not be so alarming, if the use of the media were having a positive impact on our lives. However, we know that this is having a catastrophic effect, strategically breaking down our value systems, institutions, political systems, nations, and families.

Author Yuval Noah Harari noted, "Governments and corporations will soon know you better than you know yourself. Belief in the idea of 'free will' has become dangerous...Liberalism is founded on the belief in human liberty. Unlike rats and monkeys, human beings are supposed to have 'free will'. This is what makes human feelings and human choices the ultimate moral and political authority in the world. Liberalism tells us that the voter knows best, that the customer is always right, and that we should think for ourselves and follow our hearts... But the main challenge it faces today comes not from fascism or communism, and not even from the demagogues and autocrats that are spreading everywhere like frogs after the rains. This time the main challenge emerges from the laboratories..."A man's value is not in his watch, but in how he spends his time.

> "Anything I do today, I regard as urgent. No man is given but so much time to accomplish whatever is his life's work. My life in particular never has stayed fixed in one position for very long. You have seen how throughout my life, I have often known unexpected drastic changes... I have less patience with someone who doesn't wear a watch than with anyone else, for this type is not time-conscious. In all our deeds, the proper value and respect for time determine success or failure."

—Malcolm X

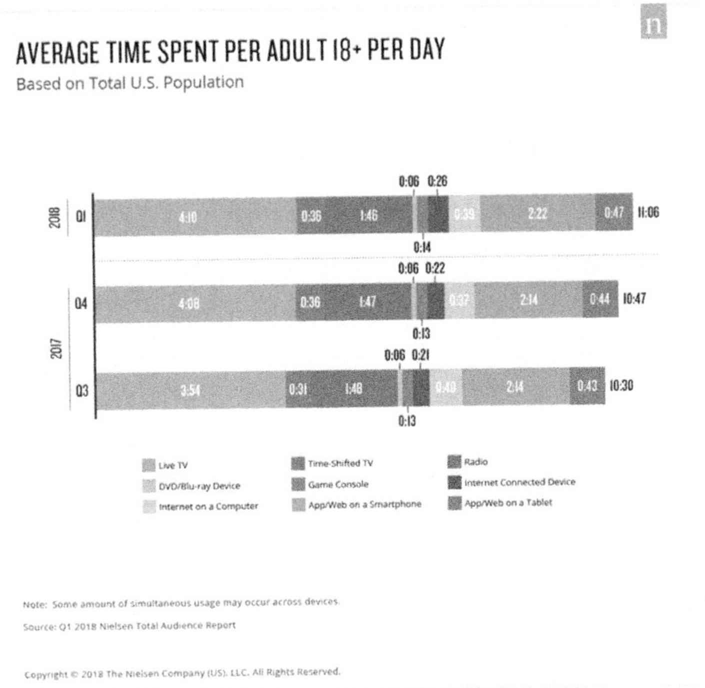
AVERAGE TIME SPENT PER ADULT 18+ PER DAY
Based on Total U.S. Population
2018
Q1
4:10
0:36
1:46
0:06
0:26
0:14
0:39
2:22
0:47
11:06
2017
Q4
4:08
0:36
1:47
0:06
0:22
0:13
0:37
2:14
0:44
10:47
Q3
3:54
0:31
1:48
0:06
0:21
0:13
0:40
2:14
0:43
10:30
Live TV
DVD/Blu-ray Device
Internet on a Computer
Time-Shifted TV
Game Console
App/Web on a Smartphone
Radio
Internet Connected Device
App/Web on a Tablet
Note: Some amount of simultaneous usage may occur across devices.
Source: Q1 2018 Nielsen Total Audience Report
Copyright © 2018 The Nielsen Company (US), LLC. All Rights Reserved.

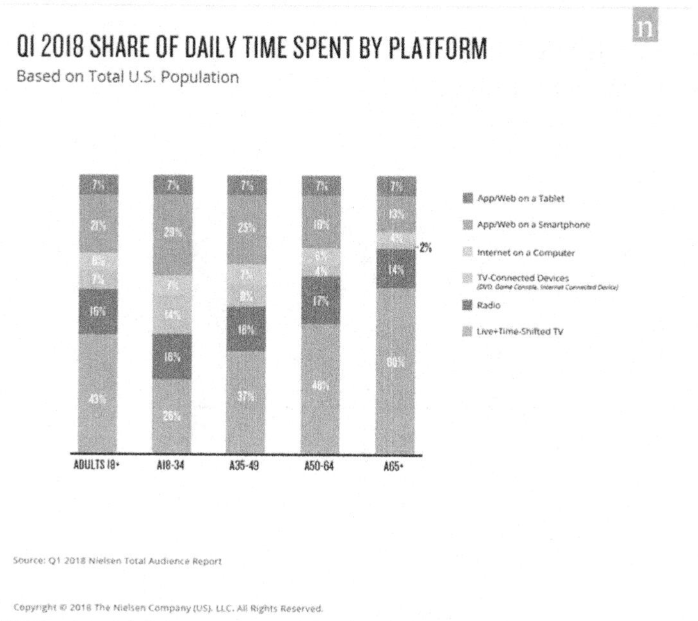
Q1 2018 SHARE OF DAILY TIME SPENT BY PLATFORM
Based on Total U.S. Population
App/Web on a Tablet
App/Web on a Smartphone
Internet on a Computer
TV-Connected Devices
Radio
Live+Time-Shifted TV
ADULTS 18+
A18-34
A35-49
A50-64
A65+
Source: Q1 2018 Nielsen Total Audience Report
Copyright © 2018 The Nielsen Company (US), LLC. All Rights Reserved.

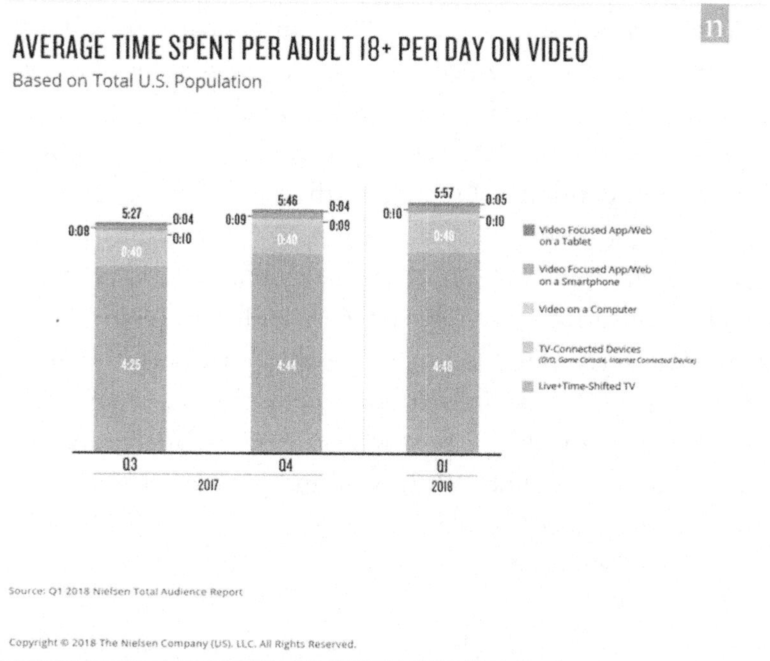
AVERAGE TIME SPENT PER ADULT 18+ PER DAY ON VIDEO
Based on Total U.S. Population
5:27
5:46
5:57
Video Focused App/Web on a Tablet
Video Focused App/Web on a Smartphone
Video on a Computer
TV-Connected Devices
Live+Time-Shifted TV
Q3
Q4
Q1
2017
2018
Source: Q1 2018 Nielsen Total Audience Report
Copyright © 2018 The Nielsen Company (US), LLC. All Rights Reserved.

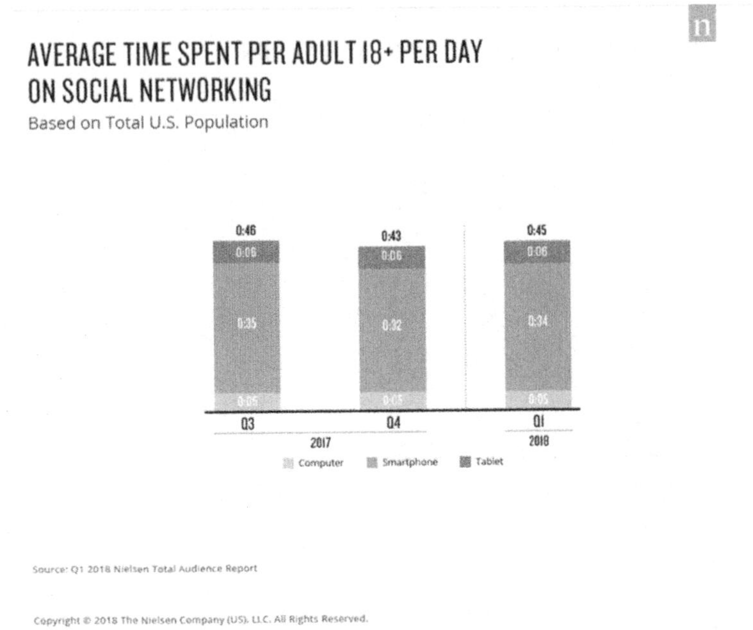


What Harari is purposing is the human animal can be hacked. Something that we all once thought was impossible. He recognizes that governments and large corporations are working diligently, to eliminate your ability to think, by doing it for you. Yuval Harari continues, "It starts with simple things. As you surf the internet, a headline catches your eye: 'Immigrant gang rapes local women'. You click on it. At exactly the same moment, your neighbor is surfing the internet too, and a different headline catches her eye: 'Trump prepares nuclear strike on Iran'. She clicks on it. Both headlines are fake news stories, generated perhaps by Russian trolls, or by a website keen on increasing traffic to boost its ad revenues. Both you and your neighbor feel that you clicked on these headlines out of your free will. But in fact you have been hacked."

Propaganda and manipulation are nothing new, of course. But whereas in the past they worked like carpet bombing, now they are becoming precision-guided munitions. When Hitler gave a speech on the radio, he aimed at the lowest common denominator, because he couldn't tailor his message to the unique weaknesses of individual brains. Now it has become possible to do exactly that. An algorithm can tell that you already have a bias against immigrants, while your neighbor already dislikes Trump, which is why you see one headline while your neighbor sees an altogether different one. In recent years some of the smartest people in the world have worked on hacking the human brain in order to make you click on ads and sell you stuff. Now these methods are being used to sell you politicians and ideologies, too. And this is just the beginning. At present, the hackers rely on analyzing signals and actions in the outside world: the products you buy, the places you visit, the words you search for online. Yet within a few years biometric sensors could give hackers direct access to your inner world, and they could observe what's going on inside your heart. Not the metaphorical heart beloved by liberal fantasies, but rather the muscular pump that regulates your blood pressure and much of your brain activity. The hackers could then correlate your heart rate with your credit card data, and your blood pressure with your search history..."

Insane, right? Ultimately these institutions would love for you to believe that you are thinking freely, but actually, they are manipulating your thought and ultimately your choices. More importantly, your most valuable resource is being stolen from you. What could you accomplish, if you use your time wisely instead of letting others spend it?

It's like being a painter with a limited amount of paint (time), and an infinite amount of everything else (opportunity). Therefore, you can paint any picture (your dream) you want on your canvas (life), however, if you are clever, you can even increase your paint, by using it judiciously. Time is your paint, and your life is your canvas. Don't waste time on things that are of little profit. Focus on the profitable and not the useless. This is something we will need to demand from creators of systems and platforms moving forward. We must focus on the benefits, but be aware of the dangers. We must ask the questions, because systems and social platforms may be safe in theory, yet extremely dangerous in practice.

Perhaps, one of the greatest lessons I have learned is that life is in the living. Whatever you want to do, do it. Whatever dream you have, live it. Whatever you see with your mind's eye, create it. Whatever your goals are, don't waste a second, be about achieving them. Life is not in the thinking or in the saying, it's in the doing. If not, others will spend your energy, time, effort, mind and life. Those that don't have a vision will spend their life serving those that have a vision. Please, don't waste another day waiting on the perfect time, which never comes. Just start, have faith, believe in God and yourself, because if you don't no one will. Spend your life and let others spend their own...

# GREED: THE SOURCE OF AMERICA'S SOCIETAL ILLS

Let America be America again.

Let it be the dream it used to be.

Let it be the pioneer on the plain
Seeking a home where he himself is free.

(America never was America to me.)

Let America be the dream the dreamers dreamed—
Let it be that great strong land of love
Where never kings connive nor tyrants scheme
That any man be crushed by one above.

(It never was America to me.)

O, let my land be a land where Liberty
Is crowned with no false patriotic wreath,
But opportunity is real, and life is free,
Equality is in the air we breathe.

(There's never been equality for me,
Nor freedom in this "homeland of the free.")

Say, who are you that mumbles in the dark?
And who are you that draws your veil across the stars?

I am the poor white, fooled and pushed apart,
I am the Negro bearing slavery's scars.

I am the red man driven from the land,
I am the immigrant clutching the hope I seek--
And finding only the same old stupid plan
Of dog eat dog, of mighty crush the weak.

I am the young man, full of strength and hope,
Tangled in that ancient endless chain
Of profit, power, gain, of grab the land!
Of grab the gold! Of grab the ways of satisfying need!
Of work the men! Of take the pay!
Of owning everything for one's own greed!

I am the farmer, bondsman to the soil.

I am the worker sold to the machine.

I am the Negro, servant to you all.

I am the people, humble, hungry, mean--
Hungry yet today despite the dream.

Beaten yet today—O, Pioneers!
I am the man who never got ahead,
The poorest worker bartered through the years.

Yet I'm the one who dreamt our basic dream
In the Old World while still a serf of kings,
Who dreamt a dream so strong, so brave, so true,
That even yet its mighty daring sings

In every brick and stone, in every furrow turned
That's made America the land it has become.

O, I'm the man who sailed those early seas
In search of what I meant to be my home—
For I'm the one who left dark Ireland's shore,
And Poland's plain, and England's grassy lea,
And torn from Black Africa's strand I came
To build a "homeland of the free."

The free?

Who said the free? Not me?
Surely not me? The millions on relief today?
The millions shot down when we strike?
The millions who have nothing for our pay?
For all the dreams we've dreamed
And all the songs we've sung
And all the hopes we've held
And all the flags we've hung,
The millions who have nothing for our pay--
Except for the dream that's almost dead today.

O, let America be America again—
The land that never has been yet—
And yet must be--the land where every man is free.

The land that's mine—the poor man's, Indian's, Negro's,
ME--
Who made America,
Whose sweat and blood, whose faith and pain,
Whose hand at the foundry, whose plow in the rain,
Must bring back our mighty dream again.

Sure, call me any ugly name you choose—
The steel of freedom does not stain.

From those who live like leeches on the people's lives,
We must take back our land again,
America!

O, yes,
I say it plain,
America never was America to me,
And yet I swear this oath—
America will be!

Out of the rack and ruin of our gangster death,
The rape and rot of graft, and stealth, and lies,
We, the people, must redeem
The land, the mines, the plants, the rivers.

The mountains and the endless plain—
All, all the stretch of these great green states—
And make America again!
—Langston Hughes

We all live in a day and time where many of us have noticed the pending hopelessness that many around us feel; it is a general air of despair. During these times many sink to the lower forms of ourselves. We begin to become even more fearful and attack those around us, those whom we don't understand. Our focus and points of view become narrow as we search for others to blame for our current predicament, failing to see how we have provided all the fuel that has carried us to this place.

We live in a time where fame and fortune have become the goal of the masses, where media have run amok through our lives, encroaching on our most private and sacred moments. Technology speeds time up, while during every waking moment corporate brands compete for our attention, as discontent in our communities continues to grow, leaving many lost, confused, and frustrated. Healthcare and education costs have become nearly unbearable for most, as we spend billions or even trillions of dollars abroad. Our school systems are lagging behind the rest of the world, when at one time they all measured themselves by us. Our safety is always being challenged, by foreign terrorist organizations, internet hackers, hate groups, local gangs, criminals, and thugs. While our politicians promise one thing and do another, we see our democratic process failing. Lobbyists and special interest groups that possess mountains of cash are drowning out the voices of the masses. Many of the middle-class jobs have been shipped away to foreign lands, only to increase some corporate entities' bottom line. While many Americans struggle to make ends meet, these corporate entities pay a lower tax rate than many middle-class families. For many, the things we are facing seem insurmountable. However, our nation has faced far greater challenges in our history than we do now, whether we look at the Great Depression or the periods before, during, and after the World Wars. The challenges were even greater. However, we met these challenges head on and we as a people weathered many storms.

Our current situations are proof of a new set of difficulties that lie before us. We must meet these challenges with optimism and a renewed hope in our possibilities as a people. All adversity presents an opportunity for great success; it has a seed of greatness on the other side of it. Remember that adversity does not test your swiftness or your strength. It tests your endurance. We find ourselves getting further and further away from the life we had and the life we have dreamed possible. Fear has set in on us all. It appears that each of us has climbed into the shell of me and mine. Very seldom is there effort to reach across lines of division, to see and understand the sameness in our struggle, to recognize that my enemy is fearful too. This conundrum lays before us a tremendous opportunity that we have at our doorstep. However, I believe the journey we must first take is within. All of us must reevaluate what we value and what type of individual we desire to be, what kind of neighborhood we want to be a part of, and what kind of country we wish to call our own. All parents must revisit what kind of future we desire for our kids and what we are teaching them to value. I am confident that we all can come to the conclusion that the status quo is not the answer.

I honestly believe that many of us are waiting for the government to provide a solution. Never in history has that assumption proved to be true. Ultimately it is the masses who will decide. In history, change appeared when one or two individuals realized the greatness that lay within them, when they decide that they would rather die standing than live on their knees. Our history books are full of such men, and they were not much different from many of us. We must banish this idea that greatness is some esoteric idea that lives beyond our reach. Often, I have found that most of us equate greatness with perfection.

> "These are two entirely different things. Perfection is thought to be the freedom from fault or defect, and greatness is very subjective to many. It depends on men's perspectives on whether someone is considered

significant or not. However, I believe that greatness lies in causes that are bigger than us. It is a spiritual realization that pushes and pulls an individual beyond the status quo. In the 60s we were faced with many of the same challenges, and found a way forward. Remember, Rome was not built in a day.

"Moreover, I am cognizant of the interrelatedness of all communities and states. I cannot sit idly by in Atlanta and not be concerned about what happens in Birmingham. Injustice anywhere is a threat to justice everywhere. We are caught in an inescapable network of mutuality, tied in a single garment of destiny. Whatever affects one directly, affects all indirectly. Never again can we afford to live with the narrow, provincial "outside agitator" idea. Anyone who lives inside the United States can never be considered an outsider anywhere within its bounds."

—Martin Luther King Jr.

This statement was used by Martin Luther King Jr., in his letter to the clergy written in the Birmingham jail. Martin was attempting to answer questions as well as appeal to the higher good of his fellow clergymen, who were very critical of the civil rights movement. Many clergymen viewed him as a rabble-rouser who needed to leave well enough alone. The clergy believed that he shouldn't be agitating the agitators; the movement should be patient and in due time things would change. King believed that the time for change was now; and anytime a man-made law, ideal or thought contradicted God's law, that law, ideal, or thought was not just and should be corrected immediately.

Amazingly, his Birmingham letter was written in April of 1963. This is some 100 years after President Lincoln issued on January 1, 1863, the final Emancipation Proclamation. With it, he officially freed all slaves within the states or parts of states that were in rebellion and not in Union hands. However, as part of Reconstruction, two new amendments were added to the Constitution. The Fourteenth Amendment, passed in June 1865, granted citizenship to all people born or naturalized in the United States. The Fifteenth Amendment, passed in February of 1869, guaranteed that no American would be denied the right to vote on the basis of race. And yet in April of 1963, Dr. King is being asked to wait for something that was nearly a hundred years overdue. Yes, all three branches of the U.S. government were complicit in withholding these rights. Throughout history, it was believed that while governments are sometimes self-absorbed, the religious institutions acted as God's police in matters of human rights, they would argue the case for the poor, broken, and forgotten. The church needed to fulfill their role as being a thermostat setting the right temperature for human rights, but it acted as a thermometer only reporting the temperature and doing little to change it. During this period it was clear that the religious institutions were in lockstep with the government. To know that the clergy stood with the three branches of U.S. Government, and not with fundamental human rights, is nothing short of breathtaking.

I know Dr. King had to be horrified to have all of the major American institutions fighting to keep the status quo. He had to have wondered, why? Well, the reason is straightforward: the civil rights movement was hurting Birmingham economically, and it threatened the economic structure of many U.S. cities and states. Imagine if every major U.S. city had a similar movement.

It would potentially destroy the economic fabric of the entire nation. This, for the clergy as well as the government, was interrupting their inward flows of cash. All financial systems need certainty to maximize profits long-term. When things are uncertain, people stop spending. The fear of this paralyzing the economic system was severe; therefore, the plan for the clergy and the government was to maintain the status quo. Well, to maintain the status quo would be to continue to perpetuate racism, which many believe to be the crux of the problem. However, racism is not what the subject of this chapter.

> "The ugliest thing in America is greed, the lust for power and domination, the lunatic ideology of perpetual Growth—with a capital G. "Progress" in our nation has for too long been confused with "Growth;" I see the two as different, almost incompatible, since progress means, or should mean, change for the better—toward social justice, a livable and open world, equal opportunity and affirmative action for all forms of life. And I mean all forms, not merely the human. The grizzly, the wolf, the rattlesnake, the condor, the coyote, the crocodile, whatever, each and every species has as much right to be here as we do."
>
> —Edward Abbey, Postcards from Ed: Dispatches and Salvos from an American Iconoclast

In essence, greed is the crux and the root from which racism stems. Greed "is an inordinate or insatiable longing, especially for wealth, status, and power." Thomas Aquinas, a philosopher, once stated that greed "is a sin against God, just as all mortal sins, in as much as man condemns things eternal for the sake of temporal thing." Meher Baba, an Indian mystic, stated that "greed is a state of restlessness of the heart, and it consists mainly of craving for power and possessions. Possessions and power are sought for the fulfillment of desires. Man is only partially satisfied in his attempt to have the fulfillment of his desires, and this partial satisfaction fans and increases the flame of craving instead of extinguishing it. Thus greed always finds an endless field of conquest and leaves the man endlessly dissatisfied. The chief expressions of greed are related to the emotional part of man."

Greed is one of the seven deadly sins. It distorts and perverts, which requires a level of blindness and self-imposed ignorance by the individual. After a while, a man's conscience will convict him and light will shine through that darkness. To continue in darkness once the sun has appeared, one would have to convince himself that his evil is somehow justified, that this is what God intended. Voila, racism; this allows him to deal with his conscience while continuing in his darkness.

At some point, systems have to be created to twist minds and pervert conscience. These corrupt systems produce ways of thinking that are passed down from generation to generation. Policies are created to provide the desired end. They come with instruction and guidelines that are there to control the results. These systems began to manufacture racism, and racism became America's best-selling product. It was taught at home, at school, at church; it became integrated into every fabric of American society. There was not one area of society that was not infected with the disease of racism. It was the dehumanization of one group so that another could justify their sins. All to cover the real culprit, economic gain, greed! I am merely suggesting that while many of us are focusing on hate, racism, and all aspects of division, the other group is running out of the back door with wealth and privilege, depriving the masses of access. They have the prosperity, and the masses have the manufactured distractions of hate, division, and poverty.

> "Declare your jihad on thirteen enemies you cannot see—egoism, arrogance, conceit, selfishness, greed, lust, intolerance, anger, lying, cheating, gossiping, and slandering. If you can master and destroy them, then you will be ready to fight the enemy you can see."
>
> —Abu Hamid Al-Ghazali

Over the last few days, after the slew of killings of defenseless African-American men and the brutal sabotage of innocent police officers, many are asking, why? How could this happen? What can we do? Let's start with a basic understanding of systems. Systems and institutions in and of themselves are not evil. Generally, they are neutral. However, they will rise or fall to the level of character of the individuals participating. It seems the masses look to government to solve all of our societal ills. In many cases, we seek legislation or a new law to somehow right a wrong. But the truth is that governments move slowly, and the wheels of justice often move even more slowly. For some strange reason we forget, a moral law carried out in an unrighteous way taints that law. It's, not just the laws. It's not the systems; it's the people. Therefore, if we want to change America, we must first change ourselves. As Gandhi said, "You must be the change you wish to see in the world." Every society has risen or fallen due to the character of its citizens; this is true for an individual, a home, a community, a state, or a country; this is also true for systems and institutions. Who are the people that are participating, and what are the instructions and guidelines for running that community?

If we return to our foundational principles and the instructional documents to the American system, then we must live up to those instructions. In Congress on July 4, 1776, our Declaration of Independence was signed into law.

"We hold these truths to be self-evident, that all men are created equal, that they are endowed by their Creator with certain unalienable Rights, that among these are Life, Liberty and the pursuit of Happiness." The committee of Benjamin Franklin, John Adams, Roger Sherman, Robert Livingston, and Thomas Jefferson, understood that this document would be the blueprint for our independence. It was created to be the navigational system of a nation. If we ever became lost, we could refer back to this document to find our way. Abraham Lincoln understood this and referred back to this in his Gettysburg Address on November 19, 1863.

> "Four score and seven years ago our fathers brought forth on this continent, a new nation, conceived in Liberty, and dedicated to the proposition that all men are created equal. Now we are engaged in a great civil war, testing whether that nation or any nation so conceived and so dedicated, can long endure. We are met on a great battle-field of that war. We have come to dedicate a portion of that field, as a final resting place for those who here gave their lives that that nation might live. It is altogether fitting and proper that we should do this. But, in a larger sense, we can not dedicate—we can not consecrate—we can not hallow—this ground. The brave

men, living and dead, who struggled here, have consecrated it, far above our poor power to add or detract. The world will little note, nor long remember what we say here, but it can never forget what they did here. It is for us the living, rather, to be dedicated here to the unfinished work which they who fought here have thus far so nobly advanced. It is rather for us to be here dedicated to the great task remaining before us—that from these honored dead we take increased devotion to that cause for which they gave the last full measure of devotion—that we here highly resolve that these dead shall not have died in vain—that this nation, under God, shall have a new birth of freedom—and that government of the people, by the people, for the people, shall not perish from the earth."

—Abraham Lincoln

"We must rapidly begin the shift from a "thing-oriented" society to a "person-oriented" society. When machines and computers, profit motives and property rights are considered more important than people, the giant triplets of racism, materialism, and militarism are incapable of being conquered."

—Martin Luther King Jr.

"Greed and selfishness are evil in all forms and have always been. Our future depends on our ability to understand the brotherhood of all mankind. We are forever linked together by God. If I ignore your circumstances, someday your circumstances will become mine. Whether I like it or not, an injustice anywhere is truly a threat to justice everywhere. Our hope lies in a return to the principles that our great nation was founded upon, and a continued reach towards the goals laid out in our founding documents. Then and only then will we fulfill the great promise of America. There are two goddesses in your head. The Goddess of Wisdom and the Goddess of Wealth. Everyone thinks they need to get wealth first, and wisdom will come. So they concern themselves with chasing money. But they have it backwards. You have to give your heart to the Goddess of Wisdom, give her all your love and attention, and the Goddess of Wealth will become jealous, and follow you."

—Joe Vigil

# THE REVEALING

"When Jesus walked the Earth, He said again and again: "Repent, for the Kingdom of Heaven is at hand." For many years I misunderstood this message. The line: "Repent, for the Kingdom of Heaven is near" brought fear because to me it meant: "Repent or else you go to hell."

But this is not what it means. Read the words again: "Repent," which means ask God for forgiveness, "because the kingdom of Heaven is at hand." which means peace is close to you.

Ask for forgiveness because when you do so in all honesty, you bring Heaven in your life. When you open your heart and ask for forgiveness in all truth, you find Heaven: the healing you need, the love you deserve, the peace you want: all of these wait for you on the other side of you having a heart-to-heart, truthful relationship with Jesus. God's love for you is unconditional, but communication is possible only in truth.

Turn your eyes from your pain, and look unto Jesus. Literally, focus your eyes on Him. Walk through the terror barrier that prevents you from opening your heart, and tell Him everything. Ask for forgiveness for everything you think you've done wrong, ask for help with your weaknesses—not from your mind or from your

> emotions, but from your spirit—and hide nothing because what you keep hidden will torment you until you bring it out to light. Carl Jung, the renowned psychiatrist said, "The most terrifying thing is to accept oneself completely." Do not be afraid. Tell God everything you fear to acknowledge, because He cannot heal what you conceal, and he will heal everything you reveal."
>
> —Dragos Bratasanu

In the mid-90's, I read a book that had a profound effect on me. The text added more clarity to things that I vaguely understood, and I had just begun the process of considering the impact of the truth on my life. The book is by James Hillman; it's called The Soul's Code: In Search of Character and Calling. It was so profound for a young man still attempting to put the pieces of his life together. The book investigates different ideas and perspectives on the origin of humanity and speaks eloquently about one's internal GPS. Plato and the Greeks called it "daimon," the Romans, "genius," the Christians, "Guardian Angel." Today we use terms such as heart, spirit, and soul. James Hillman describes it in great detail through his "Acorn Theory," in which he proposes that each life is formed by a particular image, an image that is the essence of that life and calls it destiny, just as a mighty oak's fate is written in the tiny acorn.

His theory spoke to me because it agreed with what I already believed. However, at the time, I lacked the courage and understanding to trust my heart above all else. What I found is that we must live from the inside out, not from the outside in. The spiritual is housed inside of the physical which is your body, knowing that once we die our body or our physical parts return to the earth. If we as humans lived in two parallel worlds, the physical and the spiritual; then the most significant and most powerful part of the individual is their spirit which is not subject to time and is the true you. Therefore, you, the spiritual you, must know all things, just as God or the universe (whichever you prefer). If I emanated from God, and he is eternal, then therefore, we must all have an eternal all-knowing spirit, also.

> "When all the souls had chosen their lives, they went before Lachesis. And she sent with each, as the guardian of his life and the fulfiller of his choice, the daimon that he had chosen."
>
> —Plato, Republic, Book X

In The Soul's Code, James Hillman likened the human experience to that of an upside-down tree, stating that our roots are in heaven and we are growing down into the earth. He toys with the idea of us being aware of what our purpose is in the Earth before we arrive here. Therefore, being aware of our calling and purpose, we assist God in selecting our parents based on their ability in assisting us in fulfilling our purpose. The Academy of Ideas noted: There is an idea, prominent among some thinkers, that we all possess a personal calling, a destiny unique to us alone. Our primary purpose in life, according to this idea, is to follow this calling and fulfill our destiny.

> "Being born, coming into this particular body, these particular parents, and in such a place, and what we call eternal circumstances… form a unity and are as it were spun together."
>
> —Plotinus

This idea has ancient origins; Plato weaved it in a mythic form in his Myth of Er. Before we are born, so the myth goes, our soul chooses a purpose for us to fulfill on earth. Before birth, we pass through the forgetful river at Lethe and, drinking from its waters, emerge into life ignorant of the fate our soul had chosen for us. We are accompanied on this Earth by a daimon, a spiritual companion, who acts as a "carrier of our destiny" and ensures we fulfill the fate our soul had chosen before birth.

The notion that a daimon accompanies us in life as a "carrier of our destiny" has a long and rich history. Heraclitus, before Plato, stated, "A man's daimon is his fate." The daimon for Heraclitus was a sort of force or indwelling law, which determined the course of one's life.

In more recent times James Hillman used the daimon to account for the urge we all feel to discover and align our life with a personal calling, unique to our individuality and interests, and which we can passionately devote our lives to.

Hillman conceived the daimon as a psychological complex or force existing in everyone, whose function is to help us find our personal calling, and provide us with the motivation to follow it.

> "In line with this idea, Robert Greene, author of the book Mastery, noted that throughout history many geniuses have spoken of a daimon, or inner voice, which accompanied them throughout life: For Napoleon Bonaparte it was his "star" that he always felt in ascendance when he made the right move. For Socrates, it was his daimon, a voice that he heard…which inevitably spoke to him in the negative—telling him what to avoid. For

> Goethe, he also called it a daimon—a kind of spirit that dwelled within him and compelled him to fulfill his destiny. In more modern times, Albert Einstein talked of a kind of inner voice that shaped the direction of his speculations. All of these are variations on what Leonardo da Vinci experienced with his own sense of fate."
>
> —Robert Greene, Mastery

For the majority of us this inner voice is most pronounced in childhood and adolescence, becoming less prominent as we age when the requirements and duties of adult life become a concrete reality: Mask Persona.

> "Among his various possible beings each man always finds one which is his genuine and authentic being. The voice, which calls him to that authentic being, is what we call "vocation." But the majority of men devote themselves to silencing that voice of the vocation and refusing to hear it. They manage to make a noise within themselves...to distract their own attention in order not to hear it; and they defraud themselves by substituting for their genuine selves a false course of life."
>
> —Jose Ortega Y Gasset

One of the reasons people silence the "voice of vocation" is due to the perceived risks of following it—one must sacrifice short-term comfort, status, and wealth, and engage in work where the outcome is uncertain. Yet to repress this inner calling is destructive, and often leads to the formation of what may be called a silent rage: "the absence, the anger, and the paralysis on the couch are all symptoms of the soul in search of a lost call to something other and beyond." (Hillman).

The individual who loses touch with their daimon becomes an empty shell of the person that could have been:

> "Present in body and absent in spirit, he lies back on the couch, shamed by his own daimon for the potentials in his soul that will not be subdued. He feels himself inwardly subversive, imagining in his passivity extremes of aggression and desire that must be suppressed. Solution: more work, more money, more drink, more weight, more things."
>
> —Hillman, The Soul's Code:
> In Search of Character and Callings

To ensure we don't decline into such a lifestyle, it is essential to tune into the call of fate that emanates from within, and learn to glimpse the inner workings of the daimon—using its signals and signs to help us live a more purposeful existence. This can be accomplished by looking back on our life and searching for a pattern amidst the apparently chaotic path our life has followed, as well as by attending to the inner voice and yearnings, often subtle, which seem to impel us toward a given direction.

> "For the daimon surprises. It crosses my intentions with its interventions, sometimes with a little twinge of hesitation, sometimes with a quick crush on someone or something. These surprises feel small and irrational; you can brush them aside; yet they also convey a sense of importance, which can make you say afterward: "Fate."""
>
> —James Hillman, The Soul's Code:
> In Search of Character and Callings

"Yet even if we find our personal calling we have the freedom to choose to follow it or ignore it. If we choose to ignore it, we can be sure our "inner voice" won't go away. It will be there whether we are aware of its presence or not, pushing us in the direction of our destiny until our final hours: A calling may be postponed, avoided, intermittently missed. It may also possess you completely. Whatever; eventually it will out. It makes its claim. The daimon does not go away."

—James Hillman,The Soul's Code:
In Search of Character and Callings

"Adolescents sense a secret, unique greatness in themselves that seeks expression. They gesture toward the heart when trying to express any of this, a significant clue to the whole affair."

—Joseph Chilton Pearce, Evolution's End

The revealing of something accentuates the fact that at a minimum, the seed of that thing must be present; to reveal is to make known, to disclose, to divulge, to lay open to view, to display or exhibit what is already there. No animal or being arrives into the Earth without everything it needs to carry it throughout life. You are enough, within you are undisclosed, un-divulged, un-revealed treasures which are priceless, that have no limits; the treasures are boundless. Some say your life is in the living. I disagree. I will suggest to you that your life is in the revealing. Many are trying to live, build, or create a life, from outside of themselves. You are no accident; some believe they are because of a story their parents told them. Wrong. You are a product of an elegant and intelligent design; you are a designer original, and everything about your life has been painstakingly planned. You do not need to live, build or create a life, your life must be revealed to you. I love how Jesus states in the Gospels, in Matthew 10:39(KJV), "He that findeth his life shall lose it, and he that loseth his life for my sake shall find it." Your fulfillment is tied to your purpose, and your purpose is why you have life. All your struggles and frustration are attempting to unlock that gift that abides on the inside of you. W.H. Auden, the English-American poet, noted: "The so-called traumatic experience is not an accident, but the opportunity for which the child has been patiently waiting, had it not occurred, it would have found another, equally trivial—in order to find a necessity and direction for its existence, in order that its life may become a serious matter." Difficulty and adversity are a necessary evil; they are not there to destroy you, but to grow you and push toward your authentic nature.

We must all be willing to take a look at our lives to see that there is nothing impossible for the one that believes. As you begin to step into the light of truth, as your paradigm shifts you will begin to see that there is organization to the pieces of your life that appears to embody disorder. Nothing has occurred in your life that can't be repaired or replaced. God is not somewhere pulling his hair out because you did something that he didn't know or expect. Remember, he is alpha and omega, the beginning and the end; it is ultimately his story. All our stories have been written, so they do not need to be created; your story is to be revealed. God sits outside of time in eternity; he has written the story of your life set in time. If you were writing a story, you would know what would take place in each character in the story, you would know when and who would pass away, who will cheat and steal, who will lie, and deceive; who will kill or murder. You would know all, because it's your story. History is his-story, all things begin and end with him. In Matthew 26: 34, "I tell you the truth," Jesus answered, "This very night, before the rooster crows, you will disown me three times." But Peter declared, "Even if I have to die with you, I will never disown you." And all the other disciples said the same. Later that night, Jesus was arrested. Of course it happened exactly the way Jesus stated it would happen. How did he know? Because, it's his story, Peter didn't know; it needed to be revealed to him. Why? It's not his story. Life is in the revealing and not in the living.

> "I don't evolve, I am "
>
> —Pablo Picasso

In God's eyes, you are not growing or evolving. Your story may be evolving, but not you. You are complete; eternity has completed the individual that is you, from the beginning you were complete, nothing missing. However, you are growing and evolving in the eyes of family and friends. Many of them have witnessed your development or your evolution from embryo to infant, to toddler, to grade school, to adolescent, to young adult, to adult and so on. In God's eyes, in the eyes of the creator, you are today who you will be ultimately. He knows your beginning and end. You are being revealed to your family and friends and ultimately the world.

> "There is neither beginning nor end to the imagination but it delights in its own seasons reversing the usual order at will."
>
> —William Carlos Williams, Kora in Hell

> "It was Karl Marx, I think, who once proposed that evolution be studied in reverse, with an eye firmly fixed on the evolved species while glancing backward for hints."
>
> —Jerome Bruner, In search of Mind

"Even before reason there is the inward movement which reaches out towards its own."

—Plotinus, III. 4.6

# THE POWER OF A THOUGHT

> "Begin noticing and being careful about keeping your imagination free of thoughts that you do not wish to materialize. Instead, initiate a practice of filling your creative thoughts to overflow with ideas and wishes that you fully intend to manifest. Honor your imaginings regardless of others seeing them as crazy or impossible."
>
> —Wayne Dyer

Many of us over the years have come to believe that our thoughts are of no consequence, as if our thoughts are independent of our lives. This notion is far from the truth. Our thought lives are the greatest predictor of our future successes and failures. We are basically a sum total of our most groveling inclinations. Most of us neglect the pure creative ability of our minds. We don't understand that if we are to produce anything the seeds of thought have to be planted, watered, enlightened, and brought to fruition through the choices we make. The sum of your thoughts is what you truly believe. Your thoughts shouldn't be limited by altitude, or be confined by longitude, but are defined by attitude.

To be an optimist is to assume that there is a viable solution despite the problem. A pessimist assumes there's not an adequate solution, no matter the problem. Many times we do not see things as they actually are, but how we perceive them. Perception is important, but so is attitude; however, our thoughts are the most important, because they are the compass that guides us.

I am made or unmade by myself. Through my thinking I fortify my success and failure. Your mind is like a garden, which may be intelligently cultivated or allowed to run wild, but whether cultivated or neglected, it must and will bring forth.

When the French philosopher René Descartes uttered his famous phrase, "Cogito Ergo Sum," "I think; therefore, I am," he revealed that our thoughts are the confirmation of our existence; it's perception. We don't see with our eyes, we see through them. We see with our minds. Our minds perceive and interpret, not our eyes. If you desire to change your life, you must change your thoughts. Your thoughts hold the boundaries of our lives. We can't go any further than our thoughts allows us. We cannot continue to think inside of our mental boundaries. We must cast off the shackles of our thoughts, think outside of our problems and the walls of its containment. We must think independently and not allow ourselves to become victims of others limited thinking. Lift your thoughts, think, imagine, and dream big, your thoughts are paramount in creating the life you truly desire. I was once asked, why is it that the lion is known as the king of the jungle? When he doesn't live there, why is he so feared? He is not the biggest, strongest, fastest, smartest, or the most vicious. Well, this was a question that I had previously wrestled with. I remember watching a show about the hunting tactics of lions and lionesses. I sat in amazement as I watched a small lion pride stalk a family of elephants. The elephants began to sense danger and their behavior started to disclose the fear and terror that they were experiencing. Many of the elephants circled their young, while others panicked and ran for it, while others were paralyzed with fear. I thought, wow, why are they panicking? They are smarter, bigger, and stronger yet they were fearful, while the lions were confident and resolute. At that moment, I understood why the lion is the king. The lion is the king because he thinks he is, and because he believes that so strongly, the elephants believe it also. The lion's confidence and the elephant's fear can be tracked back to their thinking. I saw the connection that thoughts are the seeds of belief and belief is manifested by confidence. Many of us never considered the importance of having a disciplined thought life and how critical it is to success. After all, our successes and failures can be traced back to our thought life. What are you thinking and why are you thinking it? Many times we fail to realize that the things we see, hear and say control our thought life. The mind is a garden and must be cared for as such. We cannot allow ourselves to become slaves of our thoughts. Our thoughts must be managed and kept free from all impurities. We must be careful about what we allow to take up space in our most creative resource, our mind. In the book, As A Man Thinketh, James Allen notes: Thought and character are one, and as character can only manifest and discover itself through environment and circumstance, the outer conditions of a person's life will always be found to be harmoniously related to his inner state. This does not mean that a man's circumstances at any given time are an indication of his entire character, but that those circumstances are so intimately connected with some vital thought-element within him that, for the time being, they are indispensable to his development… It is pleasing to human vanity to believe that one suffers because of one's virtue; but not until a man has extirpated every sickly, bitter, and impure thought from his mind, and washed every sinful stain from his soul, can he be in a position to know and declare that his sufferings are the result of his good, and not of his bad qualities; and on the way to that supreme perfection, he will have found working in his mind and life, the Great Law which is absolutely just, and which cannot give good for evil, evil for good. Possessed of such knowledge, he will then know, looking back upon his past ignorance and blindness, that his life is, and always was, justly ordered, and that all his past experiences, good and bad, were the equitable outworking of his evolving, yet un-evolved self... A man does not come to the almshouse or the jail by the tyranny of fate or circumstance, but by the pathway of groveling thoughts and base desires. Nor does a pure-minded man fall suddenly into crime by stress of any mere external force; the criminal thought had long been secretly fostered in the heart, and the hour of opportunity revealed its gathered power. Circumstance does not make the man; it reveals him to himself. No such conditions can exist as descending into vice and its attendant sufferings apart from vicious inclinations; or ascending into virtue and its pure happiness without the continued cultivation of virtuous aspirations; and man, therefore, as the lord and master of thought, is the maker of himself, the shaper and author of environment. Even at birth, the soul comes to its own, and through every step of its earthly pilgrimage, it attracts those combinations of conditions which reveal itself, which are the reflections of its own purity and impurity, its strength and weakness. Men do not attract that which they want, but that which they are. Their whims, fancies, and ambitions are thwarted at every step, but their inmost thoughts and desires are fed with their own food, be it foul or clean. The "divinity that shapes our ends" is in ourselves; it is our very Self. Man is manacled only by himself. Thought and action are the jailers of Fate—they imprison, being base; they are also the angels of Freedom—they liberate, being noble. Not what he wishes and prays for does a man get, but what he justly earns. His wishes and prayers are only gratified and answered when they harmonize with his thoughts and actions... Men are anxious to improve their circumstances, but are unwilling to improve themselves; they, therefore, remain bound. The man who does not shrink from self-crucifixion can never fail to accomplish the object upon which his heart is set. This is as true of earthly as of heavenly things. Even the man whose sole object is to acquire wealth must be prepared to make great personal sacrifices before he can accomplish his object; and how much more so he who would realize a strong and well-poised life? Here is a man who is wretchedly poor. He is extremely anxious that his surroundings and home comforts should be improved, yet all the time he shirks his work and considers he is justified in trying to deceive his employer on the ground of the insufficiency of his wages. Such a man does not understand the simplest rudiments of those principles which are the basis of true prosperity, and is not only totally unfitted to rise out of his wretchedness, but is actually attracting to himself a still deeper wretchedness by dwelling in, and acting out, indolent, deceptive, and unmanly thoughts. Here is a rich man who is the victim of a painful and persistent disease as the result of gluttony. He is willing to give large sums of money to get rid of it, but he will not sacrifice his gluttonous desires. He wants to gratify his taste for rich and unnatural viands and have his health as well. Such a man is totally unfit to have health because he has not yet learned the first principles of a healthy life… A man only begins to be a man when he ceases to whine and revile, and commences to search for the hidden justice which regulates his life. And as he adapts his mind to that regulating factor, he ceases to accuse others as the cause of his condition, and builds himself up in strong and noble thoughts; ceases to kick against circumstances, but begins to use them as aids to his more rapid progress, and as a means of discovering the hidden powers and possibilities within himself. Law, not confusion, is the dominating principle in the universe; justice, not injustice, is the soul and substance of life; and righteousness, not corruption, is the molding and moving force in the spiritual government of the world. This being so, man has but to right himself to find that the universe is right, and during the process of putting himself right, he will find that as he alters his thoughts toward things and other people, things and other people will alter toward him. The proof of this truth is in every person, and it therefore admits of easy investigation by systematic introspection and self-analysis. Let a man radically alter his thoughts, and he will be astonished at the rapid transformation it will effect in the material conditions of his life. Men imagine that thought can be kept secret, but it cannot; it rapidly crystallizes into habit, and habit solidifies into circumstance. Bestial thoughts crystallize into habits of drunkenness and sensuality, which solidify into circumstances of destruction and disease: impure thoughts of every kind crystallize into enervating and confusing habits, which solidify into distracting and adverse circumstances: thoughts of fear, doubt, and indecision crystallize into weak, unmanly, and irresolute habits, which solidify into circumstances of failure, indigence, and slavish dependence: lazy thoughts crystallize into habits of uncleanliness and dishonesty, which solidify into circumstances of foulness and beggary: hateful and condemnatory thoughts crystallize into habits of accusation and violence, which solidify into circumstances of injury and persecution: selfish thoughts of all kinds crystallize into habits of self-seeking, which solidify into circumstances more of less distressing.

I recall a story in the Bible concerning the Children of Israel; this story is one of my favorites because it holds so many truths within it that I often return to this scripture for insights and direction in my life. An evil Egyptian Pharaoh who had sworn not to release them had enslaved the Children of Israel. As the story goes, Moses was an Israelite, but by a twist of fate and circumstance had been raised as an Egyptian, and as the Pharaoh's son. One day Moses witnessing an Egyptian guard handling an Israelite roughly; he intervened, killing the Egyptian, so he ran away into the desert to hide. The latter part of the story is about a group of slaves that were being led by Moses who in turn was being led by God. After 40 years God shows up in the form of a burning bush and gives Moses his assignment to lead the Israelites out of captivity to a promised land that flows with milk and honey. Well, Moses was ordered by God to go to Pharaoh and tell him to let his people go. Pharaoh resisted, and God eventually forced his hand, and he temporarily relented before changing his mind and pursuing Moses and the Israelites into the wilderness. God performed many miracles throughout their journey to provide for an ungrateful people who became increasingly frustrated with the journey. Fast forward: now God and Moses had led them through unfathomable victories, and they are now outside of the Promised Land. So, Moses sends in 12 spies to scout out the land, to see what they would be up against in an impending battle. On their return the spies give their report, in Numbers 13:27: This is what they reported to Moses:

> 27 And they told him, and said, we came unto the land whither thou sentest us, and surely it floweth with milk and honey, and this is the fruit of it.
>
> 28 Nevertheless the people be strong that dwell in the land and the cities are walled, and very great: and moreover, we saw the children of Anak there.
>
> 29 The Amalekites dwell in the land of the south: and the Hittites, and the Jebusites, and the Amorites, dwell in the mountains: and the Canaanites dwell by the sea, and by the coast of Jordan.

> 30 And Caleb stilled the people before Moses, and said, Let us go up at once, and possess it, for we are well able to overcome it.
>
> 31 But the men that went up with him said, we are not able to go up against the people, for they are stronger than we.
>
> 32 And they brought up an evil report of the land which they had searched unto the children of Israel, saying, The land, through which we have gone to search it, is a land that eateth up the inhabitants thereof; and all the people that we saw in it are men of a great stature.
>
> 33 And there we saw the giants, the sons of Anak, which come of the giants: and we were in our own sight as grasshoppers, and so we were in their sight.

There were two of the spies, Joshua and Caleb, who believed they could win and gave a report contrary to the others. Why? You would think they saw the same things. However, the truth of our mind and thoughts are on full display here. We do not see with our eyes. We see through our eyes; we see with our minds. One group stipulated their inferiorities and stated we are like grasshoppers compared to them; this statement disclosed their thoughts about themselves, not the opinion of the inhabitants of the Promised Land. They had flawed thinking which produced erroneous views. Your ideas matter, and we must be diligent in the up-keep of our thoughts and minds. Ultimately, it will be the deciding factor on whether you will be successful or not. For me, managing my thoughts was pivotal in changing the trajectory of many situations I was facing. I had to uproot my evil thoughts with positive ones. I had to repeat over and over to myself what I wanted my mind to think and my ability to overcome adversity. Often, I have had to begin a process of reprogramming my mind with positive and winning thoughts, replacing those negative narratives that would limit my progress. After all, all that we are can be traced back to a thought. Everything that you see here on earth, had to begin with a thought. The power of a thought is incalculable, because within it is unlimited power. It is the ultimate creative ability therefore anything you desire, first needs to be conjured by your imagination, if possible there, it is possible everywhere. However, the power of your imagination can free you from containment, although that same imagination can create boundaries that can become nearly impossible to break.

When you're gifted with the power of thought
it is a wonderful thing in a way,
but it can also create problems
if your thoughts tend to go astray.
The power of thought brings things to light
That we tend to postpone
But now folks with the power of thoughts
Have today become quite known
So if you posses the power of thought
And don't know how to use it
Consult others who have the same quality, but seldom abuse it.
For the Lord gave us the power of thought
To do with as we choose
So hang on to it, always,

"It is one power you don't want to lose!"

—Norman Van Horne

"The mind is a wonderful servant but a terrible master."
—Robin S. Sharma

If we could possibly comprehend, how powerful our thoughts are, then you would never think a negative thought again. Our minds are powerful and within our thoughts is a creative ability that allows our thoughts to produce our life. I recall a story a read from a website called inspirational stories. The story begins with a man traveling to paradise and once he arrived. He sat down under the desire tree (there is such tree in the paradise, sitting under which you can immediately fulfill any your desire, you just need to think about it) and thought: "I am hungry, so it would be nice to have a bite right now." And when he just thought about this, a table full of different dishes that he was thinking about appeared right before him.

> Wow!—The man was surprised,—but it can't be!—He thought so, and the table with dishes disappeared immediately. "It would be nice to get it back!"—And dishes appeared again.
>
> He ate a plenty of dishes—he has never eaten such tasty food before. After satisfying hunger he thought: it would be nice to drink something—and a perfect wine appeared immediately, because there are no restrictions in the paradise."
>
> Lying in the shadow of the tree and drinking wine, he started wondering: Why these miracles do happen? It just can't be that everything would be so good— probably some ghosts played a joke on me.

Suddenly the ghosts appeared. They were terrible and looked like he imagined them.

The man became scared and thought: now they will kill me!

And they killed him.

Everyone lives in the world that he deserves. You are the master of your fate. Don't blame others; neither can you blame God, or the universe. Blame should be removed from your vocabulary because it has no use in your life. Your predicament is a cumulative effect of your thoughts, choices, and actions. Whatever you are and whoever you may become, you are the author, the creator, or the architect. The thoughts you have matter, the words you speak matter, your choices matter, your actions matter, they are the building blocks of your life. Thoughts are powerful so choose them wisely because eventually you will become as your thoughts are. This statement has been eternally true: "as a man thinketh, so is he."

# THE EVER CHANGING PARADIGM

The word paradigm is generally known to be a term associated with science. A scientific paradigm is a framework containing all the commonly accepted views about a subject; conventions about what direction research should take. It is a distinct set of concepts or thought patterns, including theories research methods, postulates, and standards for what constitute legitimate contributions to a field. However, outside of science a paradigm is a standard, perspective, or set of ideas, a way of looking at, understanding or perceiving something, the term was initially used by Thomas Kuhn a well-known U.S. born physicist historian and some call a philosopher who penned the groundbreaking book, The Structure Of Scientific Revolutions. This book gave us the popular term "paradigm shift," which is often used but very seldom understood. As John Naughton, a writer for the Guardian, puts it:

> The real measure of Kuhn's importance, however, lies not in the infectiousness of one of his concepts but in the fact that he singlehandedly changed the way we think about mankind's most organized attempt to understand the world. Before Kuhn, our view of science was dominated by philosophical ideas about how it ought to develop ("the scientific method"), together with a heroic narrative of scientific progress as "the addition of new truths to the stock of old truths, or the increasing approximation of theories to the truth, and in the odd case, the correction of past errors," as the Stan-

> ford Encyclopedia of Philosophy puts it. Before Kuhn, in other words, we had what amounted to the Whig interpretation of scientific history, in which past researchers, theorists and experimenters had engaged in a long march, if not towards "truth," then at least towards greater and greater understanding of the natural world.

Kuhn's version of how science develops differed dramatically from the Whig version. Where the standard account saw steady, cumulative "progress," he saw discontinuities—a set of alternating "normal" and "revolutionary" phases in which communities of specialists in particular fields are plunged into periods of turmoil, uncertainty and angst. These revolutionary phases—for example the transition from Newtonian mechanics to quantum physics—correspond to great conceptual breakthroughs and lay the basis for a succeeding phase of business as usual. The fact that his version seems unremarkable now is, in a way, the greatest measure of his success. But in 1962 almost everything about it was controversial because of the challenge it posed to powerful, entrenched philosophical assumptions about how science did—and should—work. If we can conceive for a moment that the world itself is not a fixed object, but an ever-evolving organism similar to all living things, then, if the universe is constantly evolving or moving, through that process there would be opportunity created, windows of time that would allow one to see things that they may have missed in the past. If this is true, then the entire universe is made of solutions and all problems are solved, but it would depend on what paradigm you are implementing. Let's take a moment to examine the components involved in the process of seeing or having vision. As we all know, we do not see with our eyes; we see through them; we actually see and produce vision with our minds. Our minds are generally made up of our memories of our various experiences in which we develop our truths. However, our experiences are a minuscule amount of data, too limited to claim to be knowledgeable, this would be the height of deception. Socrates compared our nature in respect to education, knowledge and its lack thereof to such an experience as described by Plato in, "The Allegory of the Cave:"

> SOCRATES: Imagined this: People live under the earth in a cave-like dwelling. Stretching a long way up toward the daylight is its entrance, toward which the entire cave is gathered. The people have been in this dwelling since childhood, shackled by the legs and neck. Thus they stay in the same place so that there is only one thing for them to look at: whatever they encounter in front of their faces. But because they are shackled, they are unable to turn their heads around.
>
> A fire is behind them, and there is a wall between the fire and the prisoners
>
> SOCRATES: Some light, of course, is allowed them, namely from a fire that casts its glow toward them from behind them, being above and at some distance. Between the fire and those who are shackled [i.e., behind their backs] there runs a walkway at a certain height. Imagine that a low wall has been built the length of the walkway, like the low curtain that puppeteers put up, over which they show their puppets.
>
> The images carried before the fire

SOCRATES: So now imagine that all along this low wall people are carrying all sorts of things that reach up higher than the wall: statues and other carvings made of stone or wood and many other artifacts that people have made. As you would expect, some are talking to each other [as they walk along] and some are silent.

GLAUCON: This is an unusual picture that you are presenting here, and these are unusual prisoners.

SOCRATES: They are very much like us humans, I [Socrates] responded.

What the prisoners see and hear

SOCRATES: What do you think? From the beginning people like this have never managed, whether on their own or with the help by others, to see anything besides the shadows that are [continually] projected on the wall opposite them by the glow of the fire.

GLAUCON: How could it be otherwise, since they are forced to keep their heads immobile for their entire lives?

SOCRATES: And what do they see of the things that are being carried along [behind them]? Do they not see simply these [namely the shadows]?

GLAUCON: Certainly.

SOCRATES: Now if they were able to say something about what they saw and to talk it over, do you not think that they would regard that which they saw on the wall as beings?

GLAUCON: They would have to.

SOCRATES: And now what if this prison also had an echo reverberating off the wall in front of them [the one that they always and only look at]? Whenever one of the people walking behind those in chains (and carrying the things) would make a sound, do you think the prisoners would imagine that the speaker were anyone other than the shadow passing in front of them?

GLAUCON: Nothing else, by Zeus!

SOCRATES: All in all, I responded, those who were chained would consider nothing besides the shadows of the artifacts as the unhidden.

GLAUCON: That would absolutely have to be.

<u>FREEDOM STAGE ONE</u>
A prisoner gets free

SOCRATES: So now, I replied, watch the process whereby the prisoners are set free from their chains and, along with that, cured of their lack of insight, and likewise consider what kind of lack of insight must be if the following were to happen to those who were chained. Walks back to the fire SOCRATES: Whenever any of them was unchained and was forced to stand up suddenly, to turn around, to walk, and to look up toward the light, in each case the person would be able to do this only with pain and because of the flickering brightness would be unable to look at those things whose shadows he previously saw.

Is questioned about the objects

SOCRATES: If all this were to happen to the prisoner, what do you think he would say if someone were to inform him that what he saw before were [mere] trifles but that now he was much nearer to beings; and that, as a consequence of now being turned toward what is more in being, he also saw more correctly?

The answer he gives

SOCRATES: And if someone were [then] to show him any of the things that were passing by and forced him to answer the question about what it was, don't you think that he would be a wit's end and in addition would consider that what he previously saw [with is own eyes] was more unhidden than what was now being shown [to him by someone else].

GLAUCON: Yes, absolutely.

Looking at the fire-light itself

SOCRATES: And if someone even forced him to look into the glare of the fire, would his eyes not hurt him, and would he not then turn away and flee [back] to that which he is capable of looking at? And would he not decide that [what he could see before without any help] was in fact clearer than what was now being shown to him?

GLAUCON: Precisely.

<u>FREEDOM, STAGE TWO</u>
Out of the cave into daylight

SOCRATES: Now, however, if someone, using force, were to pull him [who had been freed from his chains] away from there and to drag him up the cave's rough and steep ascent and not to let go of him until he had dragged him out into the light of the sun…

Pain, rage, blindness

SOCRATES: …would not the one who had been dragged like this feel, in the process, pain and rage? And when he got into the sunlight, wouldn't his eyes be filled with the glare, and wouldn't he thus be unable to see any of the things that are now revealed to him as the unhidden?

GLAUCON: He would not be able to do that at all, at least not right away.

Getting used to the light

SOCRATES: It would obviously take some getting accustomed, I think, if it should be a matter of taking into one's eyes that which is up there outside the cave, in the light of the sun.

Shadows and reflections

SOCRATES: And in this process of acclimatization he would first and most easily be able to look at (1) shadows and after that (2) the images of people and the rest of things as they are reflected in water.

Looking at things directly

SOCRATES: Later, however, he would be able to view (3) the things themselves [the beings, instead of the dim reflections]. But within the range of such things, he might well contemplate what there is in the heavenly dome, and this dome itself, more easily during the night by looking at the light of the stars and the moon, [more easily, that is to say,] than by looking at the sun and its glare during the day.

GLAUCON: Certainly

<u>FREEDOM, STAGE THREE: THE SUN</u>
Looking at the sun itself

SOCRATES: But I think that finally he would be in the condition to look at (4) the sun itself, not just at its reflection whether in water or wherever else it might appear, but at the sun itself, as it is in and of itself and in the place proper to it and to contemplate of what sort it is.

GLAUCON: It would necessarily happen this way.
Thoughts about the sun: its nature and functions

SOCRATES: And having done all that, by this time he would also be able to gather the following about the sun: (1) that it is that which grants both the seasons and the years; (2) it is that which governs whatever there is in the now visible region of sunlight; and (3) that it is also the cause of all those things that the people dwelling in the cave have before they eyes in some way or other.

GLAUCON: It is obvious that he would get to these things—the sun and whatever stands in its light—after he had gone out beyond those previous things, the merely reflections and shadows.

Thoughts about the cave

SOCRATES: And then what? If he again recalled his first dwelling, and the "knowing" that passes as the norm there, and the people with whom he once was chained, don't you think he would consider himself lucky because of the transformation that had happened and, by contrast, feel sorry for them?

GLAUCON: Very much so.

What counts for "wisdom" in the cave?

SOCRATES: However, what if among the people in the previous dwelling place, the cave, certain honors and commendations were established for whomever most clearly catches sight of what passes by and also best remembers which of them normally is brought by first, which one later, and which ones at the same time? And what if there were honors for whoever could most easily foresee which one might come by next? What would the liberated prisoner now prefer?

SOCRATES: Do you think the one who had gotten out of the cave would still envy those within the cave and would want to compete with them who are esteemed and who have power? Or would not he or she much rather wish for the condition that Homer speaks of, namely "to live on the land [above ground] as the paid menial of another destitute peasant?" Wouldn't he or she prefer to put up with absolutely anything else rather than associate with those opinions that hold in the cave and be that kind of human being?

GLAUCON: I think that he would prefer to endure everything rather than be that kind of human being.

PART THREE: THE PRISONER RETURNS TO THE CAVE

The return: blindness

SOCRATES: And now, I responded, consider this: If this person who had gotten out of the cave were to go back down again and sit in the same place as before, would he not find in that case, coming suddenly out of the sunlight, that his eyes ere filled with darkness?

GLAUCON: Yes, very much so.

The debate with the other prisoners

SOCRATES: Now if once again, along with those who had remained shackled there, the freed person had to engage in the business of asserting and maintaining opinions about the shadows—while his eyes are still weak and before they have readjusted, an adjustment that would require quite a bit of time—would he not then be exposed to ridicule down there? And would they not let him know that he had gone up but only in order to come back down into the cave with his eyes ruined—and thus it certainly does not pay to go up.

And the final outcome:

SOCRATES: And if they can get hold of this person who takes it in hand to free them from their chains and to lead them up, and if they could kill him, will they not actually kill him?

GLAUCON: They certainly will. The allegory of the cave, in many ways, describes our condition when our mind's eye has been developed by our experiences alone, When we have become firm in our own truth instead of seeking the truth, when a paradigm has become our prison that leaves us trapped in a world that has no light, only darkness, where everything we see is only a shadow of what's true and authentic. We must suffer the pain in order to condition our mind's eye to the bright light of truth. Initially the sun and the light blinds you, where you cannot see, however because of your new reality your paradigm begins to shift and brings objects (answers) into focus that you could not see before. How one can conclude they are correct due to their lim-

> ited perspective, but the frustration one must feel who has seen the light, and has to return to the cave, and to have discussion with someone that never have known freedom from their mental bondage.

Ultimately, within the Allegory of the Cave, we see the dilemma close up. The individual that is courageous enough to continue the journey, to the point of staring into the sun will forever be out of lockstep with those that remain within the cave. So this dilemma intensifies; the majority of the people in the cave will be in constant conflict with the sun gazer; a few will take heed to his experience and begin their personal journey towards truth. However, the majority will fight; they will anchor themselves inside of their truth and conclude that the sun gazer is some kind of lunatic that has been set loose to torment them. Over time the majority will begin to allow their frustration to metastasize into an all-consuming hate, which leads the majority to kill the sun gazer. In hopes that by killing him they have destroyed the truth, however truth will forever be present, no matter what lie the masses adhere to. Yes, it is forever present, it is the alpha and omega, the beginning and the end of a matter. No amount of deceit or blood can cover it, as Rudyard Kipling noted in his poem "The Legend Of Truth":

Once on a time, the ancient legends tell,
Truth, rising from the bottom of her well,
Looked on the world, but, hearing how it lied,
Returned to her seclusion horrified.
There she abode, so conscious of her worth,
Not even Pilate's Question called her forth,
Nor Galileo, kneeling to deny
The Laws that hold our Planet 'neath the sky.

Meantime, her kindlier sister, whom men call
Fiction, did all her work and more than all,
With so much zeal, devotion, tact, and care,
That no one noticed Truth was otherwhere.

Then came a War when, bombed and gassed and mined,
Truth rose once more, perforce, to meet mankind,
And through the dust and glare and wreck of things,
Beheld a phantom on unbalanced wings,
Reeling and groping, dazed, dishevelled, dumb,
But semaphoring direr deeds to come.

Truth hailed and bade her stand; the quavering shade
Clung to her knees and babbled, "Sister, aid!
I am – I was – thy Deputy, and men
Besought me for my useful tongue or pen
To gloss their gentle deeds, and I complied,
And they, and thy demands, were satisfied.
But this –" she pointed o'er the blistered plain,
Where men as Gods and devils wrought a main–
"This is beyond me! Take thy work again."

Tablets and pen transferred, she fled afar,
And Truth assumed the record of the War...
She saw, she heard, she read, she tried to tell
Facts beyond precedent and parallel–
Unfit to hint or breathe, much less to write,
But happening every minute, day and night.
She called for proof. It came. The dossiers grew.
She marked them, first, "Return. This can't be true."
Then, underneath the cold official word:
"This is not really half of what occurred."

She faced herself at last, the story runs,
And telegraphed her sister: "Come at once.
Facts out of hand. Unable overtake
Without your aid. Come back for Truth's own sake!
Co-equal rank and powers if you agree.
They need us both, but you far more than me!"

William Cullen Bryant said it this way in his poem
"The Battlefield": Truth, crushed to earth, shall rise again;
The eternal years of God are hers;
But Error, wounded, writhes with pain,
And dies among his worshippers…

Yes, "Truth crushed to the ground will rise again." Truth has won before the battle has even begun. Remember, it is forever present no matter what deceit we conjure to hide it. As you see now, ignorance and deception are not helpful, they are destroyers of all good things. Think of paradigms as you do a lens or eye glasses that further reveal what's already there. Whenever there is a problem, perhaps it is not a problem at all; it only requires a shift in your paradigm. However, this requires flexibility in mind and thought and a hunger for the truth. We can be sure of this one thing: paradigms will continue to shift, moving us closer and closer to the truth we seek. Even if you choose deception today, truth will forever be present for the ones who are willing to challenge the status quo by switching their paradigm in pursuit of truth.

# MONEY IS NOT THE ISSUE, YOU ARE...

"For the love of money is the root of all evil..."
—1 Timothy 6:10

Every month, Julia and her cousins would go for the big family meal at their grandparents' house. They would always wait excitedly for the moment their grandfather would give them a few coins, "so you can buy yourself something." Then all the children would run off to buy chewing gum, lollies, or wine gums. The grandparents, aunts, uncles, and parents commented that, behaving like this, the children would never learn to manage their money. So they proposed a special test, in which the children would have to show, over the course of a year, just what they could manage to get with those few coins.Some of the children thought that they would save their money, but Ruben and Nico, the two smallest kids, paid no attention, and they continued spending it all on sweets. Every time, they would show off their sweets in front of the other children, laughing and making fun of their cousins. They made Clara and Joe so angry that these two could no longer stand to keep saving their money. They joined Ruben and Nico in spending whatever they had, as soon as possible, on sweets.

Monty was a clever boy, and he decided to start managing his money by exchanging it: buying and selling things, or betting it with other children, in card games.

Soon he had surprised the whole family. He had accumulated a lot of money for little effort. The way he was going, he would end up almost a rich man. However, Monty was not being very careful, and he got involved in more and more risky deals. A few months later he hadn't a single penny left, after placing a losing bet on a horse race. Alex, on the other hand, had a will of iron. He saved and saved all the money he was given, wanting to win the competition, and at the end of the year he had collected more money than anyone. Even better, with so much money, he managed to buy sweets at a reduced price, so that on the day of the competition he was presented with enough sweets for much more than a year. And even then, he still had enough left over for a toy. He was the clear winner, and the rest of his cousins learnt from him the advantages of knowing how to save and how to wait.There was also Julia. Poor Julia didn't enjoy the day of the competition, because even though she had had a wonderful secret plan, she had spent her money without giving her plan enough time to work. However, she was so sure that her plan was a good one, that she decided to carry on with it, and maybe change the expressions on her relatives' faces, who had seemed to be saying, "What a disaster that girl is. She couldn't manage to save anything." When she was about to complete the second year of her plan, Julia surprised everyone by turning up at the grandparents' house with a violin and a lot of money. What was even more impressive was hearing her play. She did it really well. Everyone knew that Julia adored the violin, even though the family couldn't afford to pay for her to have lessons. So Julia had got to know a poor violinist who played in the park, and she offered him all the coins her grandfa-

> ther had given her, if he would teach her how to play. Although it wasn't much money, on seeing Julia's excitement, the violinist agreed, and he taught her happily for months. Julia showed so much desire and interest that a little after a year the violinist loaned her a violin so they could play together in the park, as a duo. They were so successful that gradually she managed to buy her own violin, with quite a bit of money to spare."
>
> —Bedtime Stories, "Grandfather's Coins"

The above story is a one that I often read to my god-children. I believe understanding money and uses should begin early.

In my profession as a Wealth Manager, I have had the opportunity to meet many people who ask me questions about their finances. However, the vast majority inquire about a stock. Within the first five minutes of the conversation, the curtain pulls back, and their real agenda becomes evident, "Give me something, inform me about an investment that can make 20% to 30% in a year." Most continue to communicate the reason why they need a 20% to 30% return, and it can be for many reasons. I need a vacation; I overpaid for my car. I need a new car; I started saving late for my retirement. My daughter is getting married; my kid is going to college; I am recently divorced; I lost my job; I took a massive loss in the last market downturn and so on and so on… All of this leaves me to conclude that many people have no real understanding of money. They don't understand what it is; how they should use it; how to save it; how to invest it; how to grow it and how to keep it. Their lack of understanding is not entirely the individual's fault, much of this has failed to be discussed in the home, school or church, and many of the financial professionals have no clue.

It's not because they don't have an education. It is because the answer to the real problem is not likely to be found in a financial, economic, or investment book, neither are the answers expected to be discussed in a macro or microeconomics course. Money is merely a medium that can be exchanged for goods and services and is used as a measure of their values on the market. Money is not evil in and of itself. Money is a tool; it is neutral, it can be used for evil or good. It serves the needs and desires of its owner. Its use rises or falls to the character level of its owner. It can act as a mirror, displaying what's right or flawed in a man's character. Money is an amplifier; it will enhance what is already there. For example, if you are a drug addict with little to no money, and somehow your cash increased, you will likely use that extra money to purchase more drugs, so the additional funds amplify the drug addiction. An increase in funds does not solve the problem. If you are a giver and that individual has a limited amount of money, and suddenly you had additional funds to give, you would likely give more money. For an evil person, more money would allow them the opportunity to do more evil. For an individual who does good, with more money, they would likely do more good. In most cases where there is a lack of money, more money would not improve the situation, and in many cases, it would likely make it worse. A lack of money is a result; it's not the cause. No matter how small the amount is, realizing you have something to work with is the beginning of thinking soberly about your finances. Very few people are born with all the money they will ever need. However, throughout our lives, many of us will have a fair amount of money that will pass through our hands, but it's what you do with it that matters. I have always believed that building wealth is often tied to a person's life philosophy; your life philosophy will determine how you would use the money. The above statement brings me to a story I heard about the Governor of California and Governor of Texas. Ever wonder about the different political and life philosophies of two of the largest states in the United States? It's apparent that California's, and Texas' leaders have different world-views. It may be a long topic of discussion, of why they differ at times. How does each state governor deal with an unexpected problem, and their respective solutions?

The Governor of California is jogging with his dog along a nature trail when suddenly a coyote jumps out and attacks him and his dog.

> #1. The Governor starts to intervene, reflects upon the movie Bambi and realizes he should stop; the coyote is only doing what comes naturally to him.
>
> #2. The Governor calls animal control. Animal control captures the coyote and spends $200 testing it for diseases, and an additional $500 to relocate it.
>
> #3. The Governor calls a veterinarian for his dog. The vet collects his dead dog and spends $200 testing it for diseases.
>
> #4. The Governor goes to the hospital and spends $3,500 getting checked for diseases from the coyote, and to get his bite wound bandaged.
>
> #5. The running trail is shut down for six months while the wildlife services conduct a $100,000 survey to make sure the area is clear of dangerous animals.

#6. The Governor spends $50,000 of state funds implementing a "coyote awareness" program for residents of the area.

#7. The State Legislature spends $2 million investigating how to handle rabies better, and how to eradicate the disease possibly.

#8. The Governor's security agent is fired for not stopping the attack and for letting the Governor intervene.

#9. The Cost: $75,000 to train a new security agent.

#10. PETA protests the coyote relocation and files suit against the state. The Governor of Texas is jogging with his dog along a nature trail when suddenly a coyote jumps out and attacks him and his dog.

#11. The Texas Governor shoots the coyote and keeps jogging. The Governor has spent $0.36 on a .380 hollow point cartridge.

The above story shows that your life philosophy can have a significant impact on your finances.

"You ought to be able to explain why you're taking the job you're taking, why you're making the investment you're making, or whatever it may be. And if it can't stand applying pencil to paper, you'd better think it through some more. And if you can't write an intelligent answer to those questions, don't do it."

—Warren Buffet

Warren Buffet's investment principles have to do more with his investment philosophy rather than strategy. One of his most powerful quotes is: "if you can not control your emotions; you can not control your money." The "Good Book" says that the love of money is the root of all evil. For many years, I have heard others recite this same passage but without the word "Love" leaving the implication that money alone is the source of all things not good. In this passage, the word "love" is critical not to leave out, because it describes an emotional connection that will ultimately lead to one's demise if omitted. Many of us blame the lack of money for a lot of the financial hardships that we experience in our everyday lives. It may be the reason that we can't take that much-needed family vacation. Why we are not able to save for retirement or contribute to our children's college fund. Or the reason why we can't put funds aside to open a business, buy a new home or donate to a cause that we care for deeply. Let's be honest with ourselves for a moment. If we look more deeply into our situations, we will find that the lack of money is a symptom and the real problem is our emotional connection to satisfy our temporary hunger. Ironically if we think about it, our brief hunger exists no matter how much money is available to us. In reality, money is neutral, a tool that we use to amplify our innermost desires. That's why a person can receive a raise on their job but continue to have the same financial struggles; living with debt and from paycheck to paycheck. Or a family can win the lottery and years later end up broke. The consensus is that more money will solve our problems but our issues have deeper roots: fear, lust, anger, grief, hunger, guilt, jealousy and yes, love for example. While watching Bloomberg, several commercials of public advisories, brokerages, and investment banks are running ads where clients are asking, why should they have to pay fees in a market downturn, or when their account has lost money. The setting for the commercial is often held in a serene place over a cup of coffee, between a father and son or husband and wife. So the son asks the father, or the wife asks the husband, do you have to pay fees when the account value is down? The father or husband turns around with a bewildered look on his face as if he is in deep thought and says good question. The whole time I am watching this, I think this is "un-believe-able." The advisory relationship is a partnership, which means that you must be willing to stay the course if you believe in the ultimate objective. You should always be sober when considering matters of money, not emotional or irrational. Anyone who gets involved in investing should understand investing and should know the numbers. I am an ex-athlete, so the competition was a necessary evil, which I love. Now, in a competitive environment, you must know your goals. Generally, you have a season, which is a set number of games. The goal is to win every game, but rarely does this happen. Therefore, you learn to turn losses into wins. First, you set smaller goals that will measure your progress with a goal of winning a championship, for example, you may discover that if you win 55% of your games, you will make the playoffs. Second, you want to ensure you turn your losses into wins by learning from your failures, to ensure that those mistakes that occurred would be eliminated by the playoffs. What if, after every loss, the players said, I want my practice time, sweat, and effort back, because it didn't work out in the previous game; or the coach was fired? This would be ridiculous. Now, the decision to move on or to fire can be made after a pattern of failure. However, you cannot get your time and money back; what you can take from this is the lesson. To train or teach people otherwise, I believe would be detrimental. In life, I have found that the majority of my failures produced great experiences that are priceless. Whatever I lost, I saw it as an exchange for the lesson. Investing in stock is ownership, which means I must go through adversity to reap in good times. I understand that experiencing losses teaches valuable lessons that are far more valuable than money or time being lost. I am convinced that if an individual got their money back every time something didn't go their way then, the failure would occur again and again. My point is, if you get that frightened during a market downturn (when there are two consecutive quarters of loss), then you shouldn't be investing. Furthermore, if you cannot shoulder a year of losses, you shouldn't be an owner, because apparently, you don't believe in the business you are participating in. Many people want to treat investing as if it's merely speculating or they treat the market like a casino. Investing is the art of ownership and the responsibility of continual learning in what makes a business successful and fruitful.

> "In its famous paradox, the equation of money and excrement, psychoanalysis becomes the first science state what common sense and the poets have long known—that the essence of money is in its absolute worthlessness."
>
> —Norman O. Brown

> "Money has never made man happy, nor will it, there is nothing in its nature to produce happiness. The more of it one has, the more one wants."
>
> —Benjamin Franklin"

> A fool and his money are soon parted."
>
> —Thomas Tusser

"Do what you love, and the money will follow."

—Marsha Sinetar

"A man with money is no match against a man on a mission."

—Doyle Brunson

"Wealth flows from energy and ideas."

—William Feather

Back in 2015, I read this article on the website Market Watch, and saved it. Not because it was something that I'd never heard before, or didn't understand, but I think many people rarely take these emotional triggers into account. In the article, "How emotions affect money habits," journalist and author Liz Weston notes: We aren't particularly rational creatures when it comes to money.

For example, my family's recent house search left me underwhelmed—until I walked into what is now our home. I stopped dead in my tracks and knew it was the place for us, even before we'd seen the kitchen or bedrooms. When that gut-deep emotion bubbled, I made the leap into buying, a decision I never regretted. What we want to avoid are emotional decisions that take us in the wrong direction. Here's how your feelings can cause you to make bad financial choices—and what to do about it. Feeling sad?

Shopping is called retail therapy for a reason. Buying stuff can make us feel better and chase away the blues, at least temporarily. The problem's when the credit card bills arrive. Sadness increases the amount of money we're willing to spend and makes us impatient, Harvard University researcher Jennifer Lerner and her colleagues found. When we're sad, we're more likely to give up a larger future benefit to have a smaller benefit right now. That's the exact opposite of the ability to delay gratification, which is what we need to save money and build wealth. Be aware when you're sad that what you really need isn't more stuff. Exercise, time spent outdoors, or hanging out with a comforting friend will provide more relief. If you can't shake your sadness, you may be suffering from depression and should seek treatment.

**When you're angry**

Angry people tend to take bigger risks and dig in their heels when their choices are questioned, refusing to admit they made a mistake. Investors do need to take some risk to make their money grow, and being stubborn can help you stick to your budget and investment goals. The trouble comes when you refuse to sell a losing stock or gamble your retirement fund by buying only highly speculative stocks.

Sometimes an objective third party, such as a fee-only financial planner, can give you the distance you need to put aside your anger and make more rational choices.

**If you are scared?**

Fear can play a big role in our financial lives. Fear of becoming a bag lady can induce us to save. Fear of leaving our loved ones impoverished can lead us to buy life insurance. It has the exact opposite effect of anger, making us exaggerate risks rather than discount them. Fear also causes us to second-guess ourselves, making us abandon a plan of action if it goes even slightly off course. For example, you may bail out of a stock when the market hits bottom(and miss the subsequent rebound). Once again, we can benefit from an experienced guide, such as a financial planner, to discuss our fears and help us stay the course.

**Feeling guilty?**

Guilt is what we feel when we violate our internal standards. If we value our family but spend too much time working, we feel guilty—and may try to make up for that with expensive presents or dinners out.

People who are more prone to guilt are also more prone to altruism. In the best-case scenario, altruism can lead us to share our abundance with others through charitable contributions. In the worse case, we can spend money we need for ourselves on others. Here is where setting limits can help. We can keep ourselves from going overboard by creating budgets for spending that can't be influenced by guilt, such as holiday presents.

**When you're thankful?**

Gratitude isn't just a pleasant emotion. Feeling thankful also "reduces excessive economic impatience," according to another Lerner study. It helps offset our tendency to discount the value of future rewards—in other words, it helps us delay gratification. So next time you're struck by the urge to spend money or dip into your savings, take a moment and list at least 10 things that make you feel grateful. You may well decide that you have more than enough. We must come to terms with the real origin of our relationship with money and what causes us to lose control of our finances. Many times the source of our money problems has nothing to do with money but has everything to do with our life philosophies. Marcel Laborde, a French financial journalist who was an acquaintance of John Maynard Keynes, an English economist, wrote Keynes a letter in 1920. He states:

> "It is self-evident that man will never be able to know what money is no more than he will be able to know what God is or the spiritual world. Money is not the infinite, an astounding complex of all sorts of psychological as well as material reactions."

Laborde is just stating that money is a result of reactions. Money is for the individual, the sum of his thoughts of money. It's difficult to define for each what money is because it depends on their perception. The creation of money exists within a legal order; it is a political act. As President Lincoln said, "Money is the creature of law, and the creation of the original issue of money should be maintained as an exclusive monopoly of the National Government." Paper money is backed by the national government; however, if there is a lack of confidence in the federal government, then money will lose its value. Paper money, without the cooperation and trust of the people using the exchange, will return to its original value—paper. 1 Timothy 6:10 says, "For the love of money is the root of all evil…" It is merely a realization that money is just paper and holds no real value of its own. But its value is granted through laws and confidence. Therefore, to love paper over people or to value it above ideas, honor, character, or loyalty, is the beginning of perversion and the root of all evil. To place your faith and confidence in a medium of exchange above all else makes the paper your source or your God. This trust is severely out of order and fosters the emotional attachments. It is the foundation of wrong thinking that allows a person to kill for it, steal for it, lie for it, cheat for it, and deceive for it. When the purpose of a thing is not known or forgotten, abuse is inevitable. Many who read this book may say that I will not kill for it or steal for it; therefore, I am okay.

However, if a lack of money in your account changes your emotional state from happy to sad, from peaceful to fearful, from secure to insecure; this is a sign that your relationship with money may be out of order. If the thought of you losing money brings you into a complete panic, where you cannot eat or sleep, perhaps your relationship with the paper is out of line. If you become enraged with a family member or friend over a $100 loan and refuse to speak to them until the debt is paid, check your relationship. Take the lesson, instead of obsessing over the $100. Only when a person places money in the proper perspective can that individual think soberly about money. If that individual stays in their emotions, then their money will manage them instead of them managing their money.

# THE NOVICE INVESTOR

"Men are anxious to improve their circumstances, but are unwilling to improve themselves; they, therefore, remain bound. The man who does not shrink from self-crucifixion can never fail to accomplish the object upon which his heart is set. This is true of earthly as of heavenly things. Even the man whose object is to acquire wealth must be prepared to make great personal sacrifices before he can accomplish his object; and how much more so he who would realize a strong and well-poised life."

—James Allen

I am gazing at the bottom of this dark rich brown leather Cigar chair that sat facing me. The Cigar chair was well worn with a rich leathery smell that draws one inward. It is rough yet refined, rugged, but yet soft. It exudes class and sophistication, with a well-worn texture that ages the chair a bit. A pair of legs that are long and never ending extending from the seat; as my eyes move upward, I notice that I am sitting across from a middle-aged man. His look is professional, but extremely tall. His forehead is lined with wrinkles as if he is in deep thought. His face is round, and his eyes are dark and piercing. His demeanor is regal with a hint of arrogance. I would say he is confident. As he crosses his long legs and continues to stare right at me, I noticed a sign of being unsure. Why is he unsure? I stared back, hoping that would get him to turn his head away. Nevertheless, the more intense my gaze became, the more he glared back at me. Our eyes were locked in on one another. The intensity of my gaze provided additional insight. As I focused in on his features the more, I understood. He is full of contradictions; he is big and powerful, yet fragile, confident, but yet unsure, thoughtful, but decisive. His grooming showed that he paid attention to details. His aura captured his spirituality and the intensity of his thoughts. The way he is glaring in my direction puts his laser focus on full display. Immediately, I realize that I must casually look to my left. Out of the corner of my eye, I notice him casually looking to his right. When I look to my right, he slowly looked to his left. It appeared he was imitating me. I smile, he smiled back; I frowned he returned my glare, I put my right hand under my chin, and immediately he put his left hand under his chin. Yes, he was mimicking my every move, because that is what mirrors do.

"Your observations and conclusions are mirrored illusions of your inner state of being, teaching you the truth through falsehoods, strength through weakness and clarity through confusion. You are seeing yourself now, disguised as the world through a lens of denial, but you will soon come to realize that what you choose to deny yourself manifests into your world. The flaws you see in your world are your most powerful teachers."

—Ka Chinery

[ … ]

To sum it up, what I put into the world comes back to me; it creates my current reality. To change my present condition, I must produce something different to create a new life-changing, result. The definition of insanity is to continue to do the same things and expecting different results. We are indeed the captains of our souls and the masters of our fate. You alone can change the trajectory of your life.

The marketplace is simply a reflection of the human experience. As an investor, one of the great lessons is that being a successful investor has as much to do with who we are, as the investment itself. Investments are at the core of our lives. In their purest form, investments are equivalent to choices. For many, money is a limited resource. Meaning that everyone will have a set amount that they are likely to earn throughout their life. Therefore, the choices you make with those earnings will have an impact on your future. In life, our most limited resource is time, and how you choose to spend or invest your time will dictate your future. To increase my time, I must spend it wisely on things that are timeless. Think of time as a seed, so I will plant that seed into relentless pursuits, into things that will last for generations. The same applies to money. I am likely to earn a set amount in my lifetime, to increase that number, I must think of it as a seed. So, I work diligently to plant/ invest into enterprises that have the likelihood to produce limitless growth opportunities. For this to be true for business, the company would need a track record of stability, profitability, adjustability, and sensibility. Those attributes are nurtured in an environment of timeless principles, character, loyalty, commitment, and service.

> The first thing you have to know is yourself. A man who knows himself can step outside himself and watch his reactions like an observer.
>
> —Adam Smith, The Money Game

Now, the same applies to the individual. The more of these attributes mentioned above one has increases their effectiveness and gives them the ability to recognize these principles in others. As Gandhi said, "You must be the change you wish to see in the world." To understand character requires us to be a person of character. To understand commitment compels us to put commitment into action. Again, the principle applies, for every action, there is an equal and opposite reaction. We cannot expect to see in our lives things that we wish not to do. Benjamin Graham said that the [sic] "the investor's chief problem and even his worst enemy is likely to be himself." Many of us deceive ourselves into believing things about ourselves that are not true. We must look into mirrors and judge our actions by the results they produce. As investors, as in life, who you are matters, and the better you know yourself, the better you will do. Know yourself, and that alone will make you a more effective investor.

Let's take a look at some of the mistakes made by many novice investors, listed by financial writer John Csiszar:

**1. Loving a Company or Stock**

Even experienced investors have companies they're passionate about for personal reasons. Their reasons can include admiration for the company's management, products or philosophy. The problem with falling in love with a certain stock is that selling it becomes much more difficult. Just because you love your smartphone, for example, doesn't mean the company's stock is a good investment.

Similarly, investors might hold on to a stock longer than appropriate. Although this problem is less likely to impact professional asset managers, experienced investors with well-managed portfolios are susceptible under the right circumstances. Some research indicates that selling a stock is typically harder for all investors than buying.

**Solution:** Practice Portfolio Discipline

To avoid the pitfall of investing in a company or stock for emotional reasons, consider putting some portfolio management rules in place. If a stock has lagged the market or dragged down your portfolio, it likely should be replaced. In general, every stock should be evaluated with the same criteria. Use discipline in this approach.

**2. Holding on to Losers**

Selling is one of the most challenging parts of successful investing mainly because stockholders believe an underperforming investment will suddenly turn around. Rather than ditching a stock after it has lost value, they continue to wait it out hoping to at least break even.

Two problems arise with this approach. First, there is typically no evidence that the stock will rebound. An investment that has tanked has demonstrated to investors only that it can go down—not the opposite. The second problem is that while investors wait for the stock to rebound, they're not invested in something more promising.

**Solution:** Look for New Investing Opportunities

Although some investments might reverse course, and some require a longer-term view, holding onto a stock based on hope usually leads to more losses.

If you wait for a stock to rebound without exploring other options, you're losing out on what's called "opportunity cost"—but it's more like an opportunity lost. Investors must consider what opportunities they're missing while they stubbornly stay in a losing investment. An investing misstep like this can be avoided by doing a regular and objective portfolio review.

**3. Missing a Plan**

A common investment maxim is "plan your trade, trade your plan." In other words, before investing a single dollar in a particular security, investors should have a plan about why they're buying it, what their profit objective is and how much they're willing to lose before declaring it a loss. Sticking to that plan after buying the stock is equally important.

**Solution:** Make and Stick to an Investment Plan

The underlying message is that even experienced investors can become emotionally involved with their trading. Setting up a trading plan gives investors rules to follow from the beginning of a trade to the end.

**4. Lacking Diversity**

Several situations can impede proper diversification. For example, employees holding company stock often run the risk of being too heavily exposed to that single investment. Alternatively, investors' best-performing stocks could become their largest holdings if they don't sell shares as they climb. Investors build diversified portfolios so that no single investment will cripple them. This is hugely important, though even experienced traders can overlook the need to rebalance their portfolios.

**Solution:** Rebalance and Diversify

Investors can avoid this common mistake by creating a schedule for rebalancing and sticking to it. Proper diversification can significantly lower a portfolio's risk factor.

**5. Timing the Market**

A big mistake made by experienced investors involves fleeing underperforming managers and chasing performance. But even great managers will underperform at times. Similarly, although timing the market is not always possible, investors must still decide which assets and asset classes to put their money in. Asset allocation is considered to be the single most important determinant of performance.

**Solution:** Don't Time the Market

Economist and Nobel Prize winner Paul Samuelson said in the Journal of Portfolio Management in 1994 that timing the market doesn't work. He said there were confident investors who moved from investing almost exclusively in stocks to the reverse based on their views of market performance.

Samuelson also determined that they don't do better over time than those who keep about 60 percent of their money in stocks and the remaining amount in bonds. There were no big moves—these investors changed their equity exposure up or down only marginally. A portfolio that's relatively independent of the overall market, and that doesn't attempt to beat a particular index, is recommended.

### 6. Overconfidence

Just as hubris drove Icarus to fly too close to the sun, overconfidence can make even a sophisticated investor think he knows better than the market. Overconfidence can blind even the most experienced investors to the signs that they are making a mistake.

**Solution:** Practice Caution

Instead of letting unfounded confidence dictate your investing moves, look to the market for data to back you up. An oft-quoted Wall Street axiom is that "the market is always right." In layman's terms, this means that even if you are 100 percent sure you are "right" in your convictions about the market going up if the market is going down, it is telling you that you are wrong.

### 7. Doubling Down

Every investor makes bad choices from time to time—it's just a fact of stock market life. A common mistake that even experienced investors make is to take a problem and make it worse by sinking more money into it. If your analysis is wrong and a stock is going down instead of up, it means you made a mistake. Doubling down and hoping to recoup your money by having a stock reverse its course is throwing good money after bad.

**Solution:** Be More Conservative

Although doubling down might work once in a while, it's not so much an investment strategy as it is playing the lottery. Be cautious—don't let your losses get the better of your decision-making.

**8. Not Seeing the Big Picture**

No investment exists in a vacuum. Even the greatest stock in the world—the tree—won't stand up if the market conditions around it—the forest—are collapsing. A perfect example is the market selloff of 2008 to 2009. Plenty of great companies got slaughtered in that bear market, trading to multi-decade or even all-time lows.

**Solution:** Take a Step Back

Many professional mutual fund managers follow investment mandates that only allow them to focus on individual stocks without adjusting for the market environment as a whole. But this usually translates to large losses when the market goes down.

If things are looking bleak for the market in general, it can be harder for your stock to succeed. On the other hand, in a booming market, even stocks without solid fundamentals are more likely to rise—a phenomenon market pundits refer to when they say, "a rising tide lifts all boats."

**9. Chasing Yield**

One of the oldest investment mistakes in the world is to "chase yield." Chasing yield refers to buying an investment because it pays an above-average yield rather than due to any fundamental analysis of the underlying investment itself. This method of investing, amounts to playing with fire because in most cases above average yields reflect an investment with higher risk.

**Solution:** Look for Consistent Yields

Managers who handle money for clients are particularly susceptible to chasing yield as they continuously strive to get higher returns for customers. But individuals are also prone to jumping at the highest number they see. Yield is computed by dividing a company's payout by its stock price. If the stock price falls dramatically, the return will skyrocket. Because a falling stock price typically represents poor business fundamentals, a company with a temporarily high yield is often a company that is about to cut its dividend.

**10. Buying Early in the Day**

The first half hour of the trading session every day is often referred to as "amateur hour." It's the time when investors either panic about overnight news or rush in to buy based on good news. Volatility is also heightened because orders piling up before the market opens are all executed at once. Experienced investors know better than to buy based on emotion—whether that emotion is fear or greed.

**Solution:** Take Your Time

It's hard to overcome human nature, even for veteran investors. Except for the last half hour of the day, the first half hour of the day typically sees the highest volume of shares traded. If there's a panic in the market, either upwards or downwards, give the market time to reach its equilibrium point before you rush in after the herd and make a mistake based on emotion.

***Bonus: Failing to Understand Behavioral Finance**

Human nature being what it is, even if you're dedicated to taking emotion out of your investing, you're likely still subject to inherent biases. Here are three of the most common behavioral tendencies affecting investors: Confirmation bias: Makes investors more likely to listen to information that reinforces preconceived notions Recent bias: Refers to the tendency to favor recent news over older news. Loss aversion: Makes investors twice as sensitive to losses as to gains.

**Solution:** Be Aware and Be Mindful

> "Although it's hard to fight human nature, failing to at least be aware of those most common behavioral tendencies can cloud your judgment when it comes to making investment decisions. Creativity doesn't come from glancing quickly at your Twitter feed while in line at Starbucks. It comes from deep thought. It comes from voraciously reading books—long books that require focused attention. It comes from meaningful discourse with other intellectually curious people. It comes from listening and asking good questions."
>
> —Joshua Rogers

One cold morning, I was sitting at my favorite coffee house, having my morning dose of java. When out of the corner of my eye I noticed an older man, reading a newspaper and sipping on a cup of coffee. Suddenly he rolled his newspaper up, and slammed it against the table, "no one knows what this damn stock market will do." I quietly thought about the words he had abruptly spoken. Was he correct? "The stock market's only reason for existing is to separate a man from his money," he railed. As I sat there, I thought about Bernard Baruch, the stockbroker, and sugar speculator, who said, "the main purpose of the stock market is to make fools of as many men as possible." Jeremy Renner, an actor, stated, "I will never be in the stock market. It's just gambling. I'm a gambler, but I'll gamble on the practicality of things." After all, was the old man's statement a fact or was this the ranting of a man who seems to be frustrated with his inability to predict the stock market accurately? Surely he knows that people win daily in the stock market, both speculators and investors. It was as if he thought that the stock market was playing a cruel trick on him. However, I must admit I have heard similar statements by many for years. I guess it is true, that what we don't understand, we criticize. What is the difference between investing and speculating? Many in the past have taken on this question; however, let's look at the two. Investing is purchasing an asset for a period of a least a year; when risk has been calculated to alleviate the potential of a total loss, with a commensurate return in mind. Speculation assumes the risk of losing 100% of funds or assets in pursuit of out-sized return, for a period of less than a year. Benjamin Graham, the author of "The Intelligent Investor," defines "an investment operation is one which, upon thorough analysis promises safety of principal and an adequate return. Operations not meeting these requirements are speculative." Mr. Graham went on to say, "We must prevent our readers from accepting the common jargon which applies the term "investor" to anybody and everybody in the stock market… in the easy language of Wall Street, everyone who buys or sells a security has become an investor, regardless of what he buys, or for what purpose, or at what price, or whether for cash or on margin. Compare this with the attitude of the public toward common stocks in 1948, when over 90% of those queried expressed themselves as opposed to the purchase of common stocks. About half gave as their reason "not safe, a gamble," and about half, the reason "not familiar with." Mr. Graham continued, "The distinction between investment and speculation in common stocks has always been a useful one, and its disappearance is a cause for concern. We have often said that Wall Street as an institution would be well advised to reinstate this distinction and to emphasize it in all its dealings with the public... What we have just said indicates that there may no longer be such a thing as a simon-pure investment policy comprising representative common stocks—in the sense that one can always wait to buy them at a price that involves no risk of a market or "quotation " loss large enough to be disquieting. In most periods the investor must recognize the existence of a speculative factor in his common-stock holdings. It is his task to keep this component within minor limits and to be prepared financially and psychologically for adverse results that may be of short or long duration. Two paragraphs should be added about stock speculation per se, as distinguished from the speculative component now inherent in most representative common stocks. Outright speculation is both, neither illegal, immoral, either (for most people) fattening to the pocketbook. More than that, some speculation is necessary and unavoidable, for in many common stock situations there are substantial possibilities of both profit and loss, and the risks therein must be assumed by someone. There is intelligent speculation as there is intelligent investing. But there are many ways in which speculation may be unintelligent. Of these the foremost are: (1) speculating when you think you are investing; (2) speculating seriously instead of as a pastime, when you lack proper knowledge and skill for it; and (3) risking more money in speculation than you can afford to lose." To understand the difference between the investor and the speculator gives us a glimpse inside the mind of the old man. Investing is a discipline and requires a disciplined approach where a true commitment to research and study is required. It is not merely a hunch, hope or a wish for a return, but a step-by-step process.

"We can easily forgive a child who is afraid of the dark; the real tragedy of life is when men are afraid of the light."

—Plato

"There is a cult of ignorance in the United States, and there has always been. The strain of anti-intellectualism has been a constant thread winding its way through our political and cultural life, nurtured by the false notion that democracy means that 'my ignorance is just as good as your knowledge."

—Isaac Asimov A flaw in one's thinking causes willful blindness.

It is a distorted perspective centered on an overemphasis on one's own thinking and experiences. Many of us start with a premise and look to find information to support that premise, instead of gathering information and looking at things from perspectives and allowing the data to build the premise. Most of us lock in on what we see and understand and somehow conclude that it is the end of the matter. We put our vision above all others, and we do this voluntarily. We cause our blindness by the confines of our limited thinking and experiences. We forget that what we thought was true at 20 becomes much different at 30 and 40, 50… Robertson Davies, a Canadian writer, stated, "A great book should be read in youth, again in maturity and once more in old age, as a fine building should be seen by morning light, at noon and by moonlight."

As we continue to collect more diverse experiences and perspectives the things we see as real, change. We all must work to eliminate our blind spots by being open to additional information and views than our own.

"It is a narrow mind which cannot look at a subject from various points of view."

—George Eliot

I sincerely hope that the older gentleman (from the coffee house) will someday understand that there is no real harm in being a novice investor, the problem occurs when you stay that way. The stock market is no arbitrary creature that does what it wants when it feels like it. It is tied to the human experience. It has its norms, its frustrations, its wins, and its losses and sometimes it can be moody or irritable. But like us at some point, it will calm and abide by more predictable rules of growth and progress. If we understand this, stay disciplined, calm and sober while keeping in mind the big picture. We too can, in the end, win at the game of investing as we often do in the game of life.

There are young men and women up and down the land who happily (or unhappily) tell anyone who will listen that they don't have an academic turn of mind, or that they aren't lucky enough to have been blessed with a good memory, and yet can recite hundreds of pop lyrics and reel off any amount of information about footballers. Why? Because they are interested in those things, they are curious. If you are hungry for food, you are prepared to hunt high and low for it. If you are hungry for information, it is the same. Information is all around us, now more than ever before in human history. You barely have to stir or incommode yourself to find things out. The only reason people do not know much is because they do not care to know. They are incurious.

Incuriosity is the oddest and most foolish failing there is.
—Stephen Fry, The Fry Chronicles

"There are two ways to be fooled. One is to believe what isn't true; the other is to refuse to believe what is true."
—Søren Kierkegaard

# WHAT'S AN INVESTMENT?

"Buffett's methodology was straightforward, and in that sense 'simple.' It was not simple in the sense of being easy to execute. Valuing companies such as Coca-Cola took a wisdom forged by years of experience; even then, there was a highly subjective element. A Berkshire stockholder once complained that there were no more franchises like Coca-Cola left. Munger tartly rebuked him. 'Why should it be easy to do something that, if done well two or three times, will make your family rich for life?"

—Roger Lowenstein, Buffett: The Making of an American Capitalist. The first step to being a successful investor is, knowing what is and isn't an investment. Warren Buffet stated in his 2011 "Berkshire Hathaway Letter to Shareholders:"

"Investing is often described as the process of laying out money now in the expectation of receiving more money in the future. At Berkshire we take a more demanding approach, defining investing as the transfer to others of purchasing power now with the reasoned expectation of receiving more purchasing power—after taxes have been paid on nominal gains in the future. More succinctly, investing is forgoing consumption now to have the ability to consume more at a later date."

From our definition there flows an important corollary: The riskiness of an investment is not measured by beta (a Wall Street term encompassing volatility and often used in measuring risk) but rather by the probability—the reasoned probability—of that investment causing its owner a loss of purchasing-power over his contemplated holding period. Assets can fluctuate greatly in price and not be risky as long as they are reasonably certain to deliver increased purchasing power over their holding period... Most believe that investments can be broken into three basic groups: ownership, lending, and cash equivalents. Ownership investments include stocks, business, real estate, precious metals; lending investments include: saving accounts and bonds; cash equivalents include: money market funds. Normally, education or consumer purchases, such as shoes, clothing, beds, cars, TVs, and anything that naturally depreciates with use and time are not investments. Investopedia explains: The reason it's not technically an investment is a practical one. For the sake of clarity, we need to avoid the added absurdity of having everything classified as an investment. We'd be "investing" every time we bought an item that could potentially make us more productive, such as investing in a stress ball to squeeze or a cup of coffee to wake you up. It is the attempt to stretch the meaning of investment to purchases, rather than education, which has obscured the meaning. I disagree with the definitions of investment given above, not because they are wrong but that the definitions are incomplete. For me, an investment is "anything" that after a period that one expects to receive a greater return in value than the value that was initially exchanged for it. All choices should be judged by which, over time, will generate the highest return. My formula for investment, and the one we use at Limitless Capital Management, is truth + idea + vision + provision (human capital, capital, intelligence) = Investment. Truth is the key to freedom and the seed of all good ideas. Ideas are the seed of vision, and vision attracts provision, which equals investment. Let's take this formula and apply it to the business founder of Apple. What was Steve Jobs' truth? What truth was the basis of his original good idea? Steve Jobs' truth was that humans are tool builders, and with tools, our excellent gifts are further enhanced.

His idea was a personal computer; his vision was a personal computer small enough to carry everywhere and was a natural extension of an individual and integrated into every facet of a person's life. His vision attracted provision (money, wealth, intelligence, human capital), which is the investment. Steve created or revealed an ecosystem, a community, a flow of uninterrupted giving and receiving.

Where there is no truth, there are no good ideas nor any vision, provision (capital), or investment.

> "Entrepreneurship is when an individual retrieves a red hot idea from the creativity furnace without the constraint of the heat of lean resources, and with each persistent blow of the innovation hammer shapes the still malleable idea against the anvil of passion, vision, insight, strategy, and principles to forge a fitting vessel of a creative concern."
>
> —Amah Lambert, Cracking the Stock Market Code: How to Make Money in Shares

> "I know quite certainly that I have no special talent. Curiosity, obsession, and dogged endurance, combined with self-criticism, have brought me to my ideas."
>
> —Albert Einstein

Einstein, in his above statement was engaged in a process that would lead him to the truth first, then to ideas. Again, an investment is "anything" after a period of time one expects to receive a greater return in value, than the value that was initially exchanged for it.

In the earlier chapters, we have spoken about the fact that money is currency, meaning, money or wealth is not to be built or stored, but it is to be revealed or created; ultimately it must flow. As we go through this process of re-evaluating our understanding of investing and discovering that alchemy does exist; one may ask, how can I create a flow or participate in alchemy? Let's take a look at the process. Socrates is one my favorite characters throughout history. For me, he is a hero, due to his relentless pursuit of wisdom and his overall opposition to the status quo. Socrates had a core set of beliefs that were not very popular in his day. He disagreed with the Sophists and their tendency to teach logic as a means of achieving selfish ends, and even more their promotion of the idea that all things are relative. To sum up relativism rather quickly, I would say that the Sophist believed that truth was relative, that you can have "a truth" based on your perspective and someone else may have a different truth based on theirs. Socrates did not believe this; he believed that there is one truth (the truth), it was the truth that he loved, desired, and believed in and would pursue until his death. Philosophy, the love of wisdom, was for Socrates itself a sacred path, a holy quest, not a game to be taken lightly. He believed, or at least said he did, in the dialog Meno (a Socratic dialog written by Plato), which contains references to the eternal body of all knowledge. We, unfortunately, lose touch with that information once we are born, because of the schism created by an eternal being entering into time. However, the eternal body of knowledge is seared upon our souls. Therefore, we need to be reminded of what we already know; we must re-discover (rather than learning something new). This is called innatism. Innatism is a philosophical and epistemological doctrine that holds that the mind is born with ideas, knowledge, and that therefore the mind is not a "blank slate" at birth. Plato and Descartes are prominent philosophers in the development of innatism and the notion that the mind is already born with ideas, knowledge, and beliefs. Both philosophers emphasize that experiences are the key to unlocking this knowledge but not the source of the knowledge itself. Essentially, no knowledge is derived exclusively from one's experiences. Although individual human beings vary due to cultural, racial, linguistic, and era-specific influences, innate ideas are said to belong to a more fundamental level of human cognition. Rene Descartes theorized that knowledge of God is innate in everybody as a product of the faculty of faith.

> "The air is full of ideas. They are knocking you in the head all the time. You only have to know what you want, then forget it, and go about your business. Suddenly, the idea will come through. It was there all the time."
>
> —Henry Ford

As we discussed in the earlier chapter "Alchemy of Finance," the finiteness of our mind has to break into bite-size pieces the vastness of the universe into past, present, and future to digest it. Remember: time (temporal, natural) sits inside the vastness of eternity (eternal, spiritual), where all things are all at once and live forever. Therefore, all experiences in the natural are subject to change, and in those experiences, the opposite experience is forever present. Socrates said that he did not teach, but rather served, like his mother, as a midwife to the truth that is already in us! Making use of questions and answers to remind his students of knowledge is called maieutic (midwifery), dialectics, or the Socratic method. I believe Socrates, Plato, and Descartes understood that learning came from information derived from experience, or information that comes from outside inward. Discernment is to differentiate, to distinguish, to perceive, which is an internal process where the information itself is derived from the inside (the eternal body of knowledge). We also see this truth displayed in the Bible, through the first man, Adam. Adam did not learn; he discerned. He didn't have to attend school to know and comprehend life's complexities; he intuitively knew. Later, in the Bible, there's a story that's in the Gospels, where Jesus was traveling with his disciples into Caesarea Philippi.

Jesus asked the disciples "Who do men say that I am?" And they said, "Some say that thou art John the Baptist: some, Elias; and others, Jeremias, or one of the prophets." He saith unto them, "But who say ye that I am?" And Simon Peter answered and said; "Thou art the Christ, the Son of the living God." And Jesus answered and said unto him, "Blessed art thou, Simon Barjona: for flesh and blood hath not revealed it unto thee, but my Father which is in heaven."

Jesus seems to be telling Peter that a human didn't teach you this; neither could he, because this was information that had not been taught, understood, nor comprehended. Peter could not grasp this information within the natural prison of his five senses. This truth lay beyond and requires a stretch, a leap of faith. Peter downloaded this information from another place, from the eternal body of knowledge of God. Think of the eternal body of all knowledge as a limitless library of blueprints. These blueprints hold the truth of the origin of all things; which allows us to see the spiritual truths that undergird the natural ones. We called them principles, which are correct in all seasons and situations. For example, the life principle "do unto others as you would have them do unto you." Over time, this will always work out better than its opposite. There are also absolutes, over time; justice is still superior to injustice, truth over a lie, character over charisma, etc. The truth about investing is that it is more of a spiritual endeavor than a natural one. It is a relentless pursuit of truth, of course, you must study and learn, but more often than not you must discern. Do not search for businesses that are profitable alone. You must go more in-depth, look for companies that you can understand their business model (blueprint) and its origins, and then you look for principles (spiritual trues) that undergird the natural ones because over time they will always win. However, time is finite and must be digested by organizing information into cycles of past, present, and future, but this library is limitless not confined by these cycles, it is, constant. Socrates had a similar understanding and shared Jesus' quest for truth. Remember, Jesus famously stated, "You shall know the truth, and it shall set you free." Truth is the key to freedom and the seed of all good ideas. Ideas are the seed of vision, and vision attracts provision, which equals investment. Therefore, first, to create or reveal a flow you must have the truth.

Social media is a revealing of ecosystem and community that always existed but needed innovation to make the invisible connections visible. Where there is no truth, there are no good ideas nor any vision, provision, or investment.

> "I know quite certainly that I have no special talent. Curiosity, obsession, and dogged endurance, combined with self-criticism, have brought me to my ideas."
>
> —Albert Einstein

Einstein, in his above statement was engaged in a process that would lead him to the truth, ideas, vision, etc. However, the answer he sought, no man had the answers. So he could not be taught or learn, to find the eternal (internal) truth, he had to rediscover, discern. Not everything is to be shown or learned; some things, the eternal ones, must be discerned. We are to live from the inside out, not from the outside in; we are not incomplete, we are complete, and have everything we need to give back to the universe that initially provided for us. Nature, the universe, God has well taken care of all living things. Lions, bears, birds, flowers, and trees all come with everything they need on the inside, and so do we. We humans are made to co-create, and through truth and ideas, our very beings are released, and the many gifts God has placed in us can be unleashed; on the inside of each of us is incredible wealth, it is limitless. How can you uncover an endless flow? You reveal an infinite stream of living from the inside out.

> "Professional investment may be likened to those newspaper competitions in which the competitors have to pick out the six prettiest faces from a hundred photographs, the prize being awarded to the competitor whose choice most nearly corresponds to the average preferences of the competitors as a whole; so that each competitor has to pick not those faces which he himself finds prettiest, but those which he thinks likeliest to catch the fancy of the other competitors, all of whom are looking at the problem from the same point of view. There is not a case of choosing neither those that, to the best of one's judgment are really the prettiest, nor even those which average opinion genuinely thinks the pretti-

est. We have reached the third degree where we devote our intelligences to anticipating what average opinion expects the average opinion to be. And there are some, I believe, who practice the fourth, fifth and higher degrees."

—John Maynard Keynes

"So to know what an investment is important. To differentiate an investment from pure speculation is necessary. To understand that investments are choices aligned with expectations is paramount to success. Always determine your risk, by ensuring that an investment is an investment or speculation wearing investment clothing. Creativity doesn't come from glancing quickly at your Twitter feed while in line at Starbucks. It comes from deep thought. It comes from voraciously reading books—long books that require focused attention. It comes from meaningful discourse with other intellectually curious people. It comes from listening and asking good questions."

—Joshua Rogers

# WHY INVEST?

> "Acknowledge the complexity of the world and resist the impression that you easily understand it. People are too quick to accept conventional wisdom, because it sounds basically true and it tends to be reinforced by both their peers and opinion leaders, many of whom have never looked at whether the facts support the received wisdom. It's a basic fact of life that many things "everybody knows" turn out to be wrong."
>
> —Jim Rogers

Many have attempted to ask this question for many different reasons. However, the most common response to the above question is to build wealth. Well, this is not the reason I invest or why I think everyone should be investing. My reason for investing is more valuable than building wealth. By the way, "to build" is antithetical to wealth or money. Wealth is to be created or revealed. Money is a currency; it is similar to water, it must flow. Money is not intended to be stored or hoarded. It is Newton's third law of motion, "For every action, there is an equal and opposite reaction." Water current occurs when opposites flow in different directions. Currents affect the Earth's climate by driving warm water from the equator and cold water from the poles around the Earth. The warm Gulf Stream, for instance, brings milder winter weather to Bergen, Norway, than to New York, much farther south. Wealth is realized when your outflows and inflows are in constant motion creating streams of income, to create inflows, something of value must be released (outflow).

Your streams must stay open to allow inflows and outflows, otherwise, the process is interrupted; it must be in a constant state of flux. I know to many this sounds strange, yet the world has operated by this principle from the beginning. The Earth's functions depend on a collaborative effort. Every living thing in some shape form or fashion depends on another. While one is giving, another is taking, and while one is taking, another is giving. Nature is in constant flux, forever changing never repeating the same moment in time again. These actions and reactions move the world forward, and generate a series of new experiences, which are derived from the measure of the action that sparks the reaction. In Matthew 7:2, KJV: "For with what judgment ye judge, ye shall be judged and with what measure ye mete, it shall be measured to you again." Every action sends out currents, and now the measure or force of that action will produce a like reaction. The Golden Rule stipulates this truth: "Do unto others as you will have them do unto you." Some say that once you've done a thing, it has already been done to you. Again, it's in a constant flux.

> "Yin and yang, male and female, strong and weak, rigid and tender, heaven and earth, light and darkness, thunder and lightning, cold and warmth, good and evil...the interplay of opposite principles constitutes the universe."
>
> —Confucius

Heraclitus of Ephesus (530-470 BC) is one of the most important thinkers in history. A Greek philosopher of the late 6th century BCE, Heraclitus criticizes his predecessors and contemporaries for their failure to see the unity in experience. He claimed to announce an everlasting Word (Logos) according to which all things are one, in some sense. Opposites are necessary for life, but they are unified in a system of balanced exchanges. The world itself consists of a law-like interchange of elements, symbolized by fire. Thus the world is not to be identified with any particular substance, but rather with an ongoing process governed by a law of change. The underlying law of nature also manifests itself as a moral law for human beings. Heraclitus was the first Western philosopher to go beyond physical theory in search of metaphysical foundations and moral applications.

Heraclitus' philosophy is a good starting point for anyone concerned with change in life. Heraclitus said that life is like a river. The peaks and troughs, pits and swirls, are all are part of the ride. Do as Heraclitus would—go with the flow. Enjoy the ride, as wild as it may be.

> Heraclitus was born into a wealthy family, but he renounced his fortune and went to live in the mountains. There, Heraclitus had plenty of opportunity to reflect on the natural world. He observed that nature is in a state of constant flux. "Cold things grow hot, the hot cools, the wet dries, the parched moistens," Heraclitus noted. Everything is constantly shifting, changing, and becoming something other to what it was before. The philosopher Plato made note of Heraclitus' ideas, "that all things go and nothing stays and comparing existents [sic] to the flow of a river, he says you could not step twice into the same river." Heraclitus believes these three things: (1) everything is constantly changing and (2) opposite things are identical, so that (3) everything is and is not at the same time. In other words, Universal Flux and the Identity of Opposites entail a denial of the

Law of Non- Contradiction. Though the waters are always changing, the rivers remain the same. Heraclitus does believe in a kind of unity of opposites. He notes, "God is day night, winter summer, war peace, satiety hunger ... As the same thing in us is living and dead, waking and sleeping, young and old. For these things have changed around are those, and conversely, those having changed around are these." Nature also further exemplifies this truth that Heraclitus has espoused. A seed is always in constant flux, changing from one form to another, yet constantly remaining the same. Of course, this seed process requires soil and water along with sunlight; each of these, soil, water, and sunlight, create opposing forces, that promotes constant change. Once the seed changes its form, it remakes and provides the seed from which it started. Think of an idea as a seed, business as the form that the idea will become, the environment where the idea is nurtured as its soil and capital as its water and proper guidance as its sun. Whether we accept this or not, our life is in constant flux; we are continuously sending things and receiving things. I believe that everyone should understand this basic premise. What I do today will affect my tomorrow, no ifs or buts about it. All investors must first have an intimate relationship with the power of choice. The investor must understand that the constant change in market conditions reveals the unity of opposites that is a foundational principle of life. Only through losses do you learn to win and through wins you learn to accept losses, however you must understand that they both exist inside of each other. Through the constant flux of losses a win reveals itself, and through a flux of wins you will find that a loss is ever present. One should never try to build wealth; wealth like value must be revealed and therefore created through the changes in conditions. Being an investor is a fact of life, now all that is left, is what kind of investor will you be. Why invest, because life itself is an investment? "But there is no energy unless there is a tension of opposites; hence it is necessary to discover the opposite to the attitude of the conscious mind."

—C.G. Jung, The Essential Jung: Selected Writings

"For the alchemist, the one primarily in need of redemption is not man, but the deity who is lost and sleeping in matter. Only as a secondary consideration does he hope that some benefit may accrue to himself from the transformed substance as the panacea, the medicine catholic, just as it may to the imperfect bodies, the base or "sick" metals, etc. His attention is not directed to his own salvation through God's grace, but to the liberation of God from the darkness of matter."

—C.G. Jung

Your dictionary.com defined alchemy as the process of taking something ordinary and turning it into something extraordinary, sometimes in a way that cannot be explained. An example of using alchemy is a person who takes a pile of scrap metal and turns it into beautiful art. When watching a movie and a wizard turns a toad into a handsome Prince, it is an example of alchemy.

Alchemy is a philosophy or science, which was popular during the Middle-Ages that experimented and repeatedly attempted to perform successful experiments of the uncommon, such as trying to turn metals into gold.

"Alchemy became part of the Greek practice of Hermeticism. You probably know that the Greek word "Hermeticism" is based on Hermes, which is the Greek name for the great Egyptian god Thoth upon whose writings the practice of Hermeticism and alchemy was based. The word "alchemy" comes from Al Khem, which means ""from the Land of Khem;" the land of Khem is a reference to Egypt."All men are by nature equal, made all of the same earth by one Workman; and however we deceive ourselves, as dear unto God is the poor peasant as the mighty prince." Plato Water: 35 liters, Carbon: 20 kg, Ammonia: 4 liters, Lime: 1.5 kg, Phosphorus: 800 g, salt: 250g, saltpeter: 100g, Sulfur: 80g, Fluorine: 7.5 g, iron: 5.6 g, Silicon: 3g, and 15 other elements in small quantities… that's the total chemical makeup of the average adult body. Modern science knows all of this, but there has never been a single example of successful human transmutation. It's like there's some missing ingredient… Scientists have been trying to find it for hundreds of years, pouring tons of money into research, and to this day they don't have a theory. For that matter, the elements found in a human being are all junk that you can buy in any market with a child's allowance. Humans are pretty cheaply made."

—Hiromu Arakawa, Fullmetal Alchemist

If you listen to your heart, you will know that it is a reality. We are limitless; have you ever thought? How can love, passion, character, loyalty, faith, and dreams be limited? Do I have a limited amount of laughs? Are my words, thoughts, acts limited? I don't believe so. These things are limitless and can be only limited by the individual. The whole process of life displays the ability of things to assume different forms. Many of the items we use daily have more than one use, many of the prescription drugs are used for something different from what they were initially created for. Life flows, and we create through that flow. Robin Sacredfire notes:

> "Our desires, dreams and hopes, open portals. These portals manifest in our conscience and five senses, in the form of decisions related to the material world but also opportunities. Now, at the same time, or maybe even slightly before in time, we get the exact opposite, the temptation, the illusion, and deception. And when we are about to make a decision, as if by magic, the two things come stronger to us, as if pushing us into a duality that makes it hard to decide. Now, this brings me to another super interesting fact: Most people assume that they have free will and that choices are hard to be made, and that life is full of dualities. And I've learned that this is just a great deception related to our planet, which, as human beings, we must transcend. And what I'm saying here is that the duality and the free will don't exist. There's only one choice to be made, the one that brings us upwards. Self-destruction is not a choice. And yet, every duality presents exactly that, and not a choice." I know that much of this can be hard to accept, especially in this day and time when much of our lives are dominated by our egos' unquenchable desires for attention. We constantly stalk social media for likes as if that somehow will justify our existence or prove our worth. Every day we roll out of bed to a job we hate to pay for a car the Jones-es will love, but our bank account will despise. Again, with the hope of disclosing our true value, well, you are enough without anyone's approval. Have you ever considered, how great men of our past

would fair in this new world of hyper-egotism, Geoffrey Miller notes: Imagine a young Isaac Newton time-traveling from 1670s England to teach Harvard under-grads in 2017. After the time-jump, Newton still has an obsessive, paranoid personality, with Asperger's syn-drome, a bad stutter, unstable moods, and episodes of psychotic mania and depression. But now he's subject to Harvard's speech codes that prohibit any "disrespect for the dignity of others"; any violations will get him in trouble with Harvard's Inquisition (the 'Office for Equity, Diversity, and Inclusion'). Newton also wants to publish Philosophic Naturalism Principia Mathematical, to ex-plain the laws of motion governing the universe. But his literary agent explains that he can't get a decent book deal until Newton builds his 'author platform' to include at least 20k Twitter followers—without provoking any backlash for airing his eccentric views on ancient Greek alchemy, Biblical cryptography, fiat currency, Jewish mysticism, or how to predict the exact date of the Apocalypse.Newton wouldn't last long as a "public in-tellectual" in modern American culture. Sooner or later, he would say "offensive" things that get reported to Harvard, and that gets picked up by mainstream media as moral-outrage click bait. His eccentric, ornery awk-wardness would lead to swift expulsion from academia, social media, and publishing. Result? On the upside, he'd drive some traffic through Huff Post, Buzzfeed, and Jezebel, and people would have a fresh controversy to virtue-signal about on Facebook. On the downside, we wouldn't have Newton's Laws of Motion."

Alchemy makes appearances throughout history, and

many have reduced it to rubbish. However, I am a firm believer in alchemy because this is a basic philosophic principle as well as a law that is at the core of all life and all things. Socrates was a believer in Alchemy not in the sense of faith but in the fact that it was a legitimate life occurrence, so were Plato, and later Aristotle convinced. I first became aware of this principle when I was a much younger man, and I was reading a dialogue between Jesus Christ and Nicodemus a Pharisee, who came to see to Jesus at night.

Immediately Jesus says to Nicodemus, "Very truly I tell you, no one can see the kingdom of God unless they are born again."

And Nicodemus asked the question that first introduced me to the possibility of Alchemy. Nicodemus speaks, "How can someone be born when they are old?" Nicodemus asked. "Surely they cannot enter a second time into their mother's womb to be born!"

Jesus' answer gave me the conclusion of the matter of Alchemy. Jesus answered, "Very truly I tell you, no one can enter the Kingdom of God unless they are born of water and the Spirit. Flesh gives birth to flesh, but the Spirit gives birth to spirit. You should not be surprised at my saying, 'You must be born again.' The wind blows wherever it pleases. You hear its sound, but you cannot tell where it comes from or where it is going. So it is with everyone born of the Spirit." We see Jesus uncovering something that we know intuitively. First, we see that things give birth after their kind; second, we see it does not have to be in the same form that it originated.

Third, we know that it may be impossible for us to quantify its original form. It is the caterpillar transforming into a butterfly. Most religious faith and scientific endeavors have transformation as a component, not because it is impossible but because it is possible. When you think about it, this is something that often happens in all our lives, you're born into the world as a baby, but over the course of your life you will be reborn many times and will take on different forms. Sometimes, who you become and where you end up will be unrecognizable compared to the place you started; yes, alchemy. The baby girl becomes a female adolescent teen, woman, wife, mother, and later grandmother. As this is occurring, she may also have been a daughter, student, friend, girlfriend, scientist, a doctor, and a Nobel Peace Prize winner. She is one person, reborn many times, taking on many different forms.

What can we quantify as new in our lives? A new pair of leather shoes is an old cow; a new home is mature trees, a new wool suit is an old sheep's wool. All are rearranged and repackaged as something new, an old thing in a new form, "alchemy." Therefore, alchemy is possible, and can be accelerated by wisdom, creativity, and innovation." Thievery pays for the tools, and the work shows me the mind of God. Stealing is a lot like alchemy, you know. In each, we each try to find what is beautiful and hidden and make it ours."

—Richard Kadrey, Sandman Slim

"Reality is merely an illusion, albeit a very persistent one."

—Albert Einstein

Poverty and lack are not real but are illusions, which through wisdom, creativity and innovation can be transformed into wealth and plenty.

What exactly did Einstein mean by the above quote and how does this apply to finance? Let's investigate... Albert Einstein did not believe that time exists in the way we perceive it. We view time in three-dimensions, past, present, and future. However, Einstein believed "time" was four-dimensional. He believed the universe was one large four-dimensional object, rather than one big three-dimensional object today and one tomorrow. Therefore, we comprehend life through experience, which is given form, by time. As Einstein said, "Time has no independent existence apart from the order of events by which we measure it."

Gevin Giorbran, the author of Everything Forever, said this of Einstein. Most everyone knows that Einstein proved that time is relative, not absolute as Newton claimed. With the proper technology, such as a very fast spaceship, one person can experience several days while another person simultaneously experiences only a few hours or minutes. The same two people can meet up again; one has experienced days or even years while the other has only experienced minutes. The person in the spaceship only needs to travel near to the speed of light. The faster they travel, the slower their time will pass relative to someone planted firmly on the Earth. If they were able to travel at the speed of light, their time would cease completely, and they would only exist trapped in timelessness…

So, the finiteness of our mind has to break into bite-size pieces the vastness of the universe into cycles of past, present, and future to digest it. Remember: time (temporal, natural) sits inside the vastness of eternity (eternal, spiritual), where all things are all at once and live forever. Therefore, all experience in the natural is subject to change, and in those experiences, the opposite experience is forever present.

> In an earlier chapter, we discussed Heraclitus, who believes in a kind of "unity of opposites." He notes, "God is day night, winter summer, war peace, satiety hunger … "As the same thing in us is living and dead, waking and sleeping, young and old. For these things have changed around are those, and conversely, those having changed around are these." King Solomon of the Old Testament who is acknowledged for his supreme wisdom was cognizant of this truth of "unity of opposites." He stated, "In the day of prosperity be joyful, but in the day of adversity consider: God also hath set the one against the other, to the end that man should find nothing after him." I also recall a story located in the New Testament about Jesus and Judas. To paraphrase the story, Judas confronts Jesus concerning a woman who was in the process of applying some costly (ointment) perfume to his feet. Judas, the traitor and treasurer (how ironic), confronts Jesus and states, "Why was not this ointment sold for three hundred pence, and given to the poor?" Jesus rebukes him and says, "… For the poor always ye have with you." At first glance, this is a mean thing to say, but I believe Jesus understood the unity of opposites. He understood poverty would forever be present as well as wealth. In every win, there is a loss present; for every truth, there is a lie present; for all wealth, poverty is forever present; for all good, evil is forever present. The "unity of opposites," and the com-

> plexity of choice, I believe each chooses what he or she will have. It is your perception and state of consciousness. I have seen victory snatched from the jaws of defeat. I have seen wealth materialize out of enormous poverty, sickness reconstituted into health, alchemy in every way. A human being is a part of the whole, called by us "Universe," a part limited in time and space. He experiences himself, his thoughts and feelings as something separated from the rest—a kind of optical delusion of his consciousness. This delusion is a prison, restricting us to our desires and affection for a few persons close to us. Our task must be to free ourselves from our prison by widening our circle of compassion to embrace all humanity and the whole of nature in its beauty.
>
> —Albert Einstein

Your finances are subject to the same rules, the same laws. Poverty and wealth are illusion conjured from our perspectives or state of consciousness that overtake our reality.

> "I have realized that the past and future are real illusions, that they exist in the present, which is what there is and all there is."
>
> —Alan Watts

Remember: poverty and lack are not real but are illusions, which through wisdom, creativity, and innovation can be transformed into wealth and plenty. We must forget the past, and future; all we have is the present and the power of choice. Change your consciousness, your perspective because the opposite is forever present. You choose.

# BOOK REFERENCE

The Limitless Approach to Life, Business, and Investments


**Truth is**

Martin Luther King, Jr. Quotes - BrainyQuote.
https://www.brainyquote.com/quotes/martin_luther_king_jr_115064

When I despair, I remember that ....
https://www.worldprayers.org/archive/prayers/meditations/when_i_despair.html

Quote by Malcolm X: "I'm for truth, no matter who tells it ....
https://www.goodreads.com/quotes/799-i-m-for-truth-no-matter-who-tells-it-i-m-for

Socrates' Triple Filter Test - Ghandchi.
http://iranscope.ghandchi.com/Fun/socrates.htm

Quote by Fyodor Dostoevsky: "Above all, don't lie to ....
https://www.goodreads.com/quotes/29218-above-all-don-t-lie-to-yourself-the-man-who-lies

Happiness Quotes (13682 quotes) - goodreads.com.
https://www.goodreads.com/quotes/tag/happiness?page=5

Nisargadatta Maharaj Quote: "It is always the false that ....
https://quotefancy.com/quote/4312/Nisargadatta-Maharaj-It-is-always-the-false-that-makes-you-suffer-the-false-desires-and

FACT CHECK: Our Deepest Fear - snopes.com.
https://www.snopes.com/fact-check/our-deepest-fear/

Quote by Muhammad Ali: "Impossible is just a big word .... https://www.goodreads.com/quotes/121663-impossible-is-just-a-big-word-thrown-around-by-small

Quote by Ayn Rand: "People think that a liar gains a .... https://www.goodreads.com/quotes/8141-people-think-that-a-liar-gains-a-victory-over-his

Quote by Henri J.M. Nouwen: "Over the years, I have come .... https://www.goodreads.com/quotes/230436-over-the-years-i-have-come-to-realize-that-the

"The truth will set you free. But not until it is finished .... https://www.goodreads.com/quotes/18719-the-truth-will-set-you-free-but-not-until-it

**The American Experiment**

Alexandre, Sandy. "Lovesick In The Time Of Smallpox: Romancing The State Of Nature In Toni Morrison's A Mercy." Criticism, vol. 59, no. 2, Wayne State University Press, Apr. 2017, p. 223.

Isaiah 43:19 KJV "Behold, I will do a new thing; now it .... https://www.kingjamesbibleonline.org/Isaiah-43-19/

PHILOSOPHICAL METHOD OF THE AMERICANS - University of Virginia. http://xroads.virginia.edu/%7EHYPER/DETOC/ch1_01.htm

God, Government and Roger Williams' Big Idea | History .... https://www.smithsonianmag.com/history/god-government-and-roger-williams-big-idea-6291280/

Historical Context: Facts about the Slave Trade and .... https://www.gilderlehrman.org/content/historical-context-facts-about-slave-trade-and-slavery

Democracy in America - Chapter X - Parties of the United .... https://americanliterature.com/author/alexis-de-tocqueville/book/democracy-in-america/chapter-x-parties-of-the-united-states

Rubén Rosario: Speech to anxious U.S. citizens in 1941 .... https://www.twincities.com/2015/12/25/ruben-rosario-speech-to-anxious-u-s-citizens-in-1941-rings-true-today/

Slavery in America - HISTORY. https://www.history.com/topics/black-history/slavery

**Ignorance Is Bliss**

The War on Knowledge: 'Ignorance is the New Intelligence .... https://www.thespoof.com/spoof-news/magazine/12334/the-war-on-knowledge-ignorance-is-the-new-intelligence

The Closing of the American Mind | The Point Magazine. https://thepointmag.com/2017/criticism/the-closing-of-the-american-mind-allan-bloom

Nihilism | Definition of Nihilism by Merriam-Webster. https://www.merriam-webster.com/dictionary/nihilism

Quote by Issac Asimov : "There is a cult of ignorance in .... https://www.goodreads.com/quotes/456687-there-is-a-cult-of-ignorance-in-the-united-states

**Inequality**

Aristotle's Constitution – Binge Thinking. https://publicphilosophyblog.com/2018/01/23/aristotles-constitution/

20 Facts About U.S. Inequality that Everyone Should Know .... https://inequality.stanford.edu/publications/20-facts-about-us-inequality-everyone-should-know

What It Means to Be Middle Class Today - Yahoo. https://www.yahoo.com/news/means-middle-class-today-130500276.html

Why Inequality Matters – Aristotle and the Middle Class .... https://underground.net/aristotle-and-the-middle-class/

20 Facts About U.S. Inequality that Everyone Should Know .... https://inequality.stanford.edu/publications/20-facts-about-us-inequality-everyone-should-know

What It Means to Be Middle Class Today - Yahoo. https://www.yahoo.com/news/means-middle-class-today-130500276.html

August | 2015 | RGT Wealth Advisors. https://rgtadvisors.com/2015/08/

Personal Finance 8/28/2014 @ 3:20PM 14,736 views Not .... https://easysite.commonwealth.com/EasySites/EasySite_H5277E/_uploads/2014-08-28-Forbes-No-Enough-People-Have-Financial-Advisors--Jamie-Hopkins-Contributor.pdf

Not Enough People Have Financial Advisers and New Research .... https://www.forbes.com/sites/jamiehopkins/2014/08/28/not-enough-people-have-financial-advisers-and-new-research-shows-they-should/

The Racial Wealth Gap: Why A Typical White Household Has .... https://www.forbes.com/sites/laurashin/2015/03/26/the-racial-wealth-gap-why-a-typical-white-household-has-16-times-the-wealth-of-a-black-one/

10 Differences Between Middle Class And Rich People .... https://loanuncle.org/blog/10-differences-middle-class-rich-people/

**Is This System Flawed**

Systems Quotes (89 quotes) - Goodreads. https://www.goodreads.com/quotes/tag/systems

Six Prison Stories | SCADP - sc-abolish.org. http://sc-abolish.org/six-prison-stories/

Education's design flaw - The Washington Post. https://www.washingtonpost.com/blogs/answer-sheet/post/educations-biggest-design-flaw/2012/07/29/gJQABxS7IX_blog.html

Theory of forms - Wikipedia. https://en.wikipedia.org/wiki/Theory_of_Forms

Men and systems. By James Allen The James Allen Free Library. http://james-allen.in1woord.nl/?text=men-and-systems

Atlas Shrugged Summary - Shmoop. https://www.shmoop.com/atlas-shrugged/summary.html

Crop rotation - Wikipedia. https://en.wikipedia.org/wiki/Crop_rotation

Men and Systems: Their Correlations and Combined Results. http://www.jamesallenlibrary.com/authors/james-allen/men-and-systems/men-and-systems-their-correlations-and-combined-results

Story Thought and System Thought – Quora Design – Medium. https://medium.com/quora-design/story-thought-and-system-thought-188dce7a87e6

**Greed**

Let America Be America Again by Langston Hughes | Poetry .... https://www.poetryfoundation.org/poems/147907/let-america-be-america-again

U.S. Postage NARFE NOTES PAID So. MD. Chapter 1260 Permit .... http://mdnarfe.org/wp-content/uploads/2018/05/NARFE-1260-NL-May-June-2018.pdf

Limitless Capital Management, Inc. LIMITLESS CAPITAL .... http://www.limitlesscapmgmt.com/blog/2016/7/20/america-the-societal-ills-continue

Social Justice Quotes (442 quotes) - Goodreads. https://www.goodreads.com/quotes/tag/social-justice

Lying Quotes (490 quotes) - Goodreads. https://www.goodreads.com/quotes/tag/lying

**The Revealing**

Carl Jung Quotes (24 quotes) - Goodreads. https://www.goodreads.com/quotes/tag/carl-jung

Daimon as Character and Calling | Meetup. https://www.meetup.com/The-Chicago-Philosophy-Meetup/events/236197001/

James Hillman: The Daimon and the Search For a Calling. https://academyofideas.com/2016/02/james-hillman-the-daimon-and-the-search-for-a-calling/

John 12:25 KJV "He that loveth his life shall lose it; and .... https://www.kingjamesbibleonline.org/John-12-25/

Matthew 26 NIV - The Plot Against Jesus - When Jesus had .... https://www.biblegateway.com/passage/?search=Matthew%2026&version=NIV

**The Power of Thought**

Begin noticing and being careful about keeping your .... https://www.brainyquote.com/quotes/wayne_dyer_718010

Effect of Thought on Circumstances - As A Man Thinketh .... http://www.sapphyr.net/largegems/asamanthinketh2.htm

NUMBERS 13:33 KJV "And they told him, and said, We came .... https://www.kingjamesbibleonline.org/Numbers-13-27/

NUMBERS 13:27 KJV "And they told him, and said, We came .... https://www.kingjamesbibleonline.org/Numbers-13-27/

Quote by Robin Sharma: "The mind is a wonderful servant .... https://www.goodreads.com/quotes/534889-the-mind-is-a-wonderful-servant-but-a-terrible-master

Inspired to inspire - Home | Facebook. https://www.facebook.com/Inspired-to-inspire-864515523580219/

**The Ever Changing Paradigm**

Thomas Kuhn: the man who changed the way the world looked .... https://www.theguardian.com/science/2012/aug/19/thomas-kuhn-structure-scientific-revolutions

Plato's Allegory of the Cave - UDL Book Builder.
http://bookbuilder.cast.org/view_print.php?book=102554

Plato THE ALLEGORY OF THE CAVE Republic , VII 514 a, 2 to ....
https://web.stanford.edu/class/ihum40/cave.pdf

Plato THE ALLEGORY OF THE CAVE Republic , VII 514 a, 2 to ....
https://web.stanford.edu/class/ihum40/cave.pdf

**Money Is Not The Issue**

Money Is Not The Issue - Limitless Capital Management, Inc..
http://www.limitlesscapmgmt.com/blog/2016/8/4/money-is-not-the-issue

MONEY IS NOT THE ISSUE - Limitless Capital Management, Inc..
http://www.limitlesscapmgmt.com/blog/2016/8/4/money-is-not-the-issue

A short story to teach kids to manage money - Bedtime Stories.
https://freestoriesforkids.com/children/stories-and-tales/grandfather's-coins

How emotions affect money habits - MarketWatch.
https://www.marketwatch.com/story/how-emotions-affect-money-habits-2015-03-13

**The Novice Investor**

The Novice Investor - Limitless Capital Management, Inc..
http://www.limitlesscapmgmt.com/blog/2016/8/12/the-novice-investor

13 Biggest Mistakes Even Experienced Investors Make ....
https://www.gobankingrates.com/investing/strategy/biggest-mistakes-investors-make/

Joshua Rogers Quotes (Author of Mauro Giuliani 120 Right ....
https://www.goodreads.com/author/quotes/7328410.Joshua_Rogers

Willful Ignorance Quotes (59 quotes) - Goodreads.
https://www.goodreads.com/quotes/tag/willful-ignorance

Warren Buffett Quotes (19 quotes) - Goodreads.
https://www.goodreads.com/quotes/tag/warren-buffett

Limitless Capital Management, Inc. LIMITLESS CAPITAL ....
http://www.limitlesscapmgmt.com/blog/2018/6/27/the-formula-of-investment

Introduction to Philosophy : Test Flashcards | Quizlet.
https://quizlet.com/202756441/introduction-to-philosophy-test-flash-cards/

What is Innatism? | Innatism Definition | Innatism Explained.
https://www.youtube.com/watch?v=0MheBT_kLC0

The General Theory of Employment, Interest and Money ....
https://en.wikipedia.org/wiki/The_General_Theory_of_Employment,_Interest_and_Money

Chapter 12: The State of Long Term Expectation.
https://washburn.edu/faculty/rweigand/page2/HWFiles/Keynes-State-of-Long-Term-Expectation.pdf

Joshua Rogers Quotes (Author of Mauro Giuliani 120 Right ....
https://www.goodreads.com/author/quotes/7328410.Joshua_Rogers

**Why Invest?**

Limitless Capital Management, Inc. LIMITLESS CAPITAL ....
http://www.limitlesscapmgmt.com/blog/2017/8/7/why-invest

Matthew 7:1-2 KJV - Judge not, that ye be not judged. For ....
https://www.biblegateway.com/passage/?search=Matthew%207:1-2&version=KJV

Heraclitus, Change, and Flow - Brewminate.
http://brewminate.com/heraclitus-change-and-flow/

Heraclitus | Internet Encyclopedia of Philosophy.
https://www.iep.utm.edu/heraclit/

New York Center for Jungian Studies JUNG 2017 Sidebar-1st ....
https://nyjungcenter.org/content-block/jung-2017-sidebar-1st-week-full/

Alchemy Quotes (156 quotes) - Goodreads.
https://www.goodreads.com/quotes/tag/alchemy

Limitless Capital Management, Inc. LIMITLESS CAPITAL ....
http://www.limitlesscapmgmt.com/blog/2017/8/8/vikaxnbwr8d16drdscu2ylsr0tktr5-s6ypo

Psychiatry Quotes (247 quotes) - goodreads.com.
https://www.goodreads.com/quotes/tag/psychiatry?page=3

Paranoid Quotes (32 quotes) - Goodreads.
https://www.goodreads.com/quotes/tag/paranoid

Exploring Real History: STONE: 11 ILLEGAL US BASES IN ....
https://exploringrealhistory.blogspot.com/2017/07/stone-11-illegal-us-bases-in.html

# ABOUT THE AUTHOR

Hello, my name is Marcus Turner. I am the Founder, CEO, and CIO of Limitless Capital Management Inc. We are a "Boutique Registered Investment Advisory," I started this company because of my lifelong passion for investing, and the great sense of satisfaction and enjoyment I feel helping people achieve peace of mind with their financial situation through financial planning, investment management, and education.

Within the American System of Capitalism, are core principles of free markets and competition. At the heart of competition, is a sense of fair play and equal opportunity. Currently here in the US and many places around the world, this is not the case. As you know billions of people around the globe need on-ramps because they are facing incalculable odds. Many start life without the proper resources necessary to live, much less to compete in a global economy. This truth allows the establishment to entrench their positions by creating and overseeing systems that benefit the few versus the many. When so many are locked out, we hold the future of humanity hostage and put a stranglehold on our children possibilities. The future of humanity depends on our ability to provide access and develop systems that will benefit all citizens of the global community.

We believe that God endowed each of us with inalienable rights and these rights include the ability to pursue happiness. No one group or geographic location has the trademark on good ideas, concepts, or intelligent designs. We must cultivate an environment where the best ideas flourish no matter where the idea originated. We must invest in our forgotten ones and prove that over time social consciousness will be more productive and profitable than the current systems that benefit the few. We must work diligently in creating a meritocracy where character, beliefs, and ideas are the deciding factor. Not those same superficial measuring sticks that brought us to this point, where the entitled continue to fortify their destructive positions while perpetuating the narrative of the haves and the have-nots. The status quo is unacceptable; we must harness the power of capital, investment, innovation, technology, creativity and love to deliver us from this conundrum. In this book, I wanted to introduce you to the principles, thinking and general information on which those beliefs are built. I sincerely hope you found "The Limitless Approach" useful.

Thank you,
Marcus A. Turner

Made in the USA
Monee, IL
04 November 2026

67384882R00125